STUDIES IN ENGL

Ge

David Daiches

Already published in the series:

Already published in the series *(continued)*:

MILTON:
PARADISE LOST

by

DAVID DAICHES

EDWARD ARNOLD

First published 1983 by
Edward Arnold (Publishers) Ltd
41 Bedford Square,
London WC1B 3DQ

Reprinted 1986

British Library Cataloguing in Publication Data

Daiches, David
  Milton: Paradise lost.
  1. Milton, John. 1608-1674. Paradise lost
  I. Title
  821'.4   PR3562

  ISBN 0-7131-6389-5

Typeset by Colset Pte Ltd, Singapore
Printed in Great Britain by
The Camelot Press Ltd, Southampton

General Preface

The object of this series is to provide studies of individual novels, plays and groups of poems and essays which are known to be widely read by students. The emphasis is on clarification and evaluation; biographical and historical facts, while they may be discussed when they throw light on particular elements in a writer's work, are generally subordinated to critical discussion. What kind of work is this? What exactly goes on here? How good is this work, and why? These are the questions that each writer will try to answer.

It should be emphasized that these studies are written on the assumption that the reader has already read carefully the work discussed. The objective is not to enable students to deliver opinions about works they have not read, nor is it to provide ready-made ideas to be applied to works that have been read. In one sense all critical interpretation can be regarded as foisting opinions on readers, but to accept this is to deny the advantages of any sort of critical discussion directed at students or indeed at anybody else. The aim of these studies is to provide what Coleridge called in another context 'aids to reflection' about the works discussed. The interpretations are offered as suggestive rather than as definitive, in the hope of stimulating the reader into developing further his own insights. This is after all the function of all critical discourse among sensible people.

Because of the interest which this kind of study has aroused, it has been decided to extend it first from merely English literature to include also some selected works of American literature and now further to include selected works in English by Commonwealth writers. The criterion will remain that the book studied is important in itself and is widely read by students.

DAVID DAICHES

Contents

Preface

Paradise Lost, Milton's long meditated epic, is not an easy work for the modern reader fully to understand and appreciate. We may admire the richness and variety of the language, the effective moulding of the sustained passages and cunning placing of pauses and the range of devices that enabled Milton to describe an ideal prelapsarian world in terms of imagery drawn from daily experience in the postlapsarian or fallen world he knew. Nevertheless, the difficulties are many. Milton, the most learned of our poets, worked in a tradition of Christian Humanism, that assumed a deep familiarity with the major documents of the Christian religion, of which the Bible was the most important, and with classical Greek and Latin literature, history and mythology. It assumed also a knowledge of human geography, both ancient and modern, and of geographical discovery and astronomical theory. Indeed, Milton can be said to have called on virtually all kinds of knowledge and of attitudes developed by biblical, classical, medieval and Renaissance man. He himself was a Renaissance man, as his treatise *Of Education* shows, believing that a properly educated citizen should have mastered 'all the offices both private and publick of Peace and War'. But he also held, as he says in the same treatise, that the aim of learning is 'to repair the ruins of our first Parents by regaining to know God aright, and out of that knowledge to love him, to imitate him, to be like him'. A Christian aim is combined with a Humanist ideal. Perhaps the only area of thought that Milton can be said to have excluded from his remarkable synthesis was the medieval Christian one of private, cloistered virtue. He had the true Protestant suspicion of the monastic ideal ('I cannot praise a fugitive and cloister'd virtue, unexercis'd and unbreath'd', he wrote in *Areopagitica*) and agreed with the Renaissance repudiation of the medieval separation of the life of contemplation and the life of action. He was perhaps the last of the great Christian Humanists, taking the classical and the Christian worlds as his joint inheritance. He also had an intimate knowledge of Italian literature from Dante to Tasso and of the way the Italian language had been used by Renaissance poets as a vehicle for poetry both lyric and epic.

All this makes difficulties for most modern readers. Milton took for granted in his readers a range of knowledge – biblical, classical, theological and other kinds – on which he drew effortlessly for imagery, reference, allusion, suggestion as well as for direct communication. Consider, for example, that splendid passage in Book IX describing Eve, having won

Adam's reluctant consent to work in another part of the garden, sliding her hand out of Adam's before going off:

> Thus saying, from her Husbands hand her hand
> Soft she withdrew, and like a Wood-Nymph light
> *Oread* or *Dryad*, or of *Delia's* Traine,
> Betook her to the Groves, but *Delia's* self
> In gate surpass'd and Goddess-like deport,
> Though not as shee with Bow and Quiver armd,
> But with such Gardning Tools as Art yet rude,
> Guiltless of fire had formd, or Angels brought.
> To *Pales*, or *Pomona* thus adornd,
> Likest she seemd, *Pomona* when she fled
> *Vertumnus*, or to *Ceres* in her Prime,
> Yet Virgin of *Proserpina* from *Jove*.

The modern reader will get the general idea, but instead of receiving the impression of Eve's beauty and bearing from the classical similes he will work in the reverse way, assuming that the characters to whom Milton compares Eve must be symbols of beauty and high bearing (in some undifferentiated way) because Eve is compared to them. The result is that he will see as mere decoration what for Milton and his first readers was not only an organic part of a poetic description but a part that enriched and concentrated with quite specific suggestions and references the impression he was trying to convey. There are numerous occasions of this kind in *Paradise Lost*, and the modern reader will often require an editorial explanatory note before he can make the effort of imagination to engage with the full resonance of the passage as Milton wrote it. Indeed, Milton's vocabulary, not only his imagery and his figures of speech, is shot through with implications and references to kinds of knowledge not readily available to most readers today.

A second reason for the difficulty of *Paradise Lost* for the modern reader is the subject. Milton wrote to 'justifie the wayes of God to men'. This does not mean that his aim was to prove in general that in spite of all human suffering God, although both all-good and all-powerful, was not responsible, but specifically it was to prove that God was both good and just in allowing Adam and Eve to be tempted to eat the forbidden fruit in the Garden of Eden and to punish all their descendants in consequence of their ancestors' disobedience. The traditional Christian justification of the ways of God to men was the theory of '*felix culpa*', the doctrine of the fortunate fall, that saw Adam's fall as necessary to bring forth new aspects of God's mercy and love in the Christian scheme of redemption. But in *Paradise Lost*, though this is referred to, it does not take a central place. The appalling history of postlapsarian man is told by the archangel Michael with bleak pessimism. By the time he wrote *Paradise Lost* Milton had no illusions about human suffering, about the wicked prospering and the unjust persecuting the just, about the ravages of illness and old age: 'So shall the world go on,/To good malignant, to bad men benign' until the Day of Judgment.

In his posthumously published Latin work on Christian Doctrine Milton audaciously proclaimed that 'many ocular demonstrations, many true predictions verified, many wonderful works have compelled all nations to believe, either that God, or some evil power whose name was unknown, presided over the affairs of the world'. This extraordinary statement shows that Milton conceded that experience suggested that the world as it is must be ruled by an evil spirit, but if we accept the Bible as God's divine revelation (which Milton certainly did) and therefore know that in fact the world is ruled by God, who is by definition good, we accept God's rule as the alternative. It remains true that the facts (as distinct from divinely revealed truth or intuitively apprehended knowledge of God's nature) cannot justify the ways of God to men, quite apart from the question of God's responsibility for the temptation of Adam and Eve and their fall. That God is both all-good and all-powerful is not reconcilable with the facts of evil and suffering that have prevailed throughout human history except by the argument from revealed religion or religious experience. Neither of these constitutes proof to those who do not accept the revealed religion as truly revealed by God or who have not undergone the appropriate religious experience. To write an epic poem to 'justifie the wayes of God to men' is therefore, to many modern readers, a somewhat paradoxical endeavour, especially as it actually shows God arguing in verse about the reconcilability of His foreknowledge with His creature man's free-will and the consequent responsibility of man for everything that he does and that happens to him as a result. A devotional poem intended to create a state of mind in which the reader comes to accept the God of love would be a more acceptable aim in the present climate of religious opinion than an epic poem that takes the Genesis story about the eating of the forbidden fruit as literally true and is designed to justify God and prove man culpable.

There is a third difficulty for the modern reader. *Paradise Lost* is an epic, a form descending from classical times, from the 'primary' epic of Homer through the 'secondary' epic of Virgil to Renaissance poets and critics and theorists who imitated it and formulated rules about it, so that by Milton's time the epic was seen as a highly stylized kind of long poem on a subject of heroic significance that demanded not only a high heroic style but also some essential conflict between opposing parties. Today we have no great interest in long poems written in a traditional mode, and this lack of interest might put off many readers of Milton, even if in fact Milton's handling of the epic tradition was in many ways revolutionary. *Paradise Lost* is the only wholly successful full-scale epic poem in English, but that is not likely to impress those who will not equip themselves properly for a reading of the poem.

So we are faced with the three-fold difficulty that *Paradise Lost* is the work of a Christian Humanist working in a Christian—classical tradition unfamiliar to most of us; that it is designed to 'justify the wayes of God to men' by reasons most modern readers find difficult to accept (even assuming the aim means anything at all); and that it is an epic, a long poem written in what is basically an ancient tradition. In spite of this, there are in the poem a richness and a humanity that transcend its declared aim and the limitations of its form. Milton has in fact produced in *Paradise Lost* a remarkable poem that explores and illuminates some of the central paradoxes of human experience. The theology and cosmology of the poem are in a sense only incidental to this achievement. The justification of the ways of God to men emerges not as the logical inference from the narrative of events, still less as the result of arguments put defensively into God's mouth, but as part of the continuing reverberations of meaning achieved by Milton through the poetic means in which he presents the story.

The reverberations of meaning operate in a great variety of ways, some of them readily discernible by the modern reader (such as the host of associations and multiple meanings set going by the word 'fruit' in the very first line of the poem, developed throughout the poem in all sorts of ways both literally and metaphorically, with trees, gardens, flowers, seed, consequences, among the many related topics), some of them operating through rhetorical devices so often discussed and categorized by Renaissance critics but now little known and less immediately appreciated. The more one reads *Paradise Lost* the more one comes to recognize Milton's mastery of his craft, his remarkable power to choose and organize language in the interests of richly evocative expression, the flow and movement of his cunningly articulated sentences that carry the reader on effortlessly yet at the same time keep firmly in control of his responses, changing his expectations of what a sentence is to be about until a great variety of alternative and mutually enriching suggestions have been allowed to develop.

To provide guidance on the biblical, classical and other allusions that Milton introduced so confidently but which today are not readily available, today's readers will do well to use an annotated modern edition. The annotations can be regarded as a preliminary clarification of the text. The real critical task is to demonstrate the ways in which Milton's poetic craftsmanship in *Paradise Lost* creates as the poem unfolds a complex of developing meaning (whether or not it justifies the ways of God to men in the ways Milton intended) that remains illuminating and moving. To do this in detail would require a most minute examination of the poem line by line and even word by word, which is beyond the scope of this study. What we shall try to do here is to provide suggestions and examples that will help the reader to see the poem as a great work of literary art that explores the complexities of the human condition more profoundly than any summary of its action could possibly suggest.

In Milton's early manhood, when his classical and his Christian inheritance lay more equally in his imagination than in his later years, when the latter more and more prevailed, he had thought of writing an epic poem on some aspect of early British history, taking a hero such as King Arthur. Then, when he had settled on the theme of *Paradise Lost*, he first thought of writing it as a drama modelled on ancient Greek tragedy. Some time in the 1650s he decided on the epic form, and he appears to have composed the poem (dictating it, for he was by then blind) between 1658 and 1663, i.e., in the last years of the Commonwealth and the first years of the Restoration, a period which saw the steady erosion of all Milton's early enthusiastic hopes of a new regenerate English commonwealth freed from royal absolutism and religious superstition, a free, Protestant community of which he would be the poet and celebrant. With the Restoration of 1660 Milton saw the definite end of all his political and religious ambitions for his country, and he retired into private life to finish his great epic that inevitably came to reflect something of his own frustrations about public affairs. How far we should read autobiographical implications into the gloomy picture of world history painted by Michael in Book XII, with its advice to Adam to seek 'a paradise within thee' rather than mourn the loss of an external one, is a matter on which critics differ. But it is not necessary to bring in Milton's biography for an understanding of what goes on in the poem, as distinct from an understanding of the reasons why Milton chose to write it the way he did. The latter question is not a literary-critical one. What we are concerned with here is the nature of Milton's epic and its quality.

There were two editions of *Paradise Lost* in Milton's lifetime, the first, divided into 10 books, in 1667, and the second, re-divided into 12 books, in 1674. It is the text of the second edition ('Revised and Augmented by the same Author') that is used here, in the original spelling.

Paradise Lost

The Beginning

Although Milton had shown himself a master of rhymed verses in his earlier poetry, he deliberately rejected rhyme for *Paradise Lost*. In 1668 he added to the copies that then remained of the first edition a note on the verse: 'The Measure is *English* Heroic Verse without Rime, as that of *Homer* in *Greek*, and of *Virgil* in *Latin*; Rime being no necessary Adjunct or true Ornament of Poem or good Verse, in longer works especially, but the Invention of a barbarous Age, to set off wretched matter and lame Meeter; . . .' He notes that 'not without cause' Italian and Spanish poets have rejected rhyme and that some of our best English tragedies are in unrhymed verse. What gives 'true musical delight' is not rhyme but 'apt Numbers, fit quantity of Syllables, and the sense variously drawn out from one Verse into another'. In achieving this aim Milton was much influenced by the diction and verse of Italian poetry, especially epic poetry, but he adapted Italian usage to the genius of the English language. His standard line has 10 syllables (while the Italian had 11), with an underlying pattern of stresses on the second, fourth, sixth, eighth and tenth. This pattern of stresses is not at all rigidly adhered to; there is a remarkable musical flexibility in the way Milton handles his lines, but the tenth syllable almost always has a stress with other stresses falling on the fourth or the sixth. Most impressive of all is Milton's skill in sustaining a whole run of lines, with varied pauses and emphases, building up suggestions, modifying them, even altering them (without altogether losing the original ones) in a rich and musical verse that echoes away in reverberating and inter-connecting meanings as the lines move on. This is what he meant by his phrase 'the sense variously drawn out from one Verse into another'. It can be seen in the magisterial opening of the poem:

> Of Mans First Disobedience, and the Fruit
> Of that Forbidden Tree, whose mortal tast
> Brought Death into the World, and all our woe,
> With loss of *Eden*, till one greater Man
> Restore us, and regain the blissful Seat,
> Sing Heav'nly Muse, that on the secret top
> Of *Oreb*, or of *Sinai*, didst inspire
> That Shepherd, who first taught the chosen Seed,
> In the Beginning how the Heav'ns and Earth
> Rose out of *Chaos*: Or if *Sion* Hill

Delight thee more, and *Siloa's* Brook that flow'd
Fast by the Oracle of God; I thence
Invoke thy aid to my adventrous Song,
That with no middle flight intends to soar
Above th' *Aonian* Mount, while it pursues
Things unattempted yet in Prose or Rhime.
And chiefly Thou O Spirit, that dost prefer
Before all Temples th' upright heart and pure,
Instruct me, for Thou know'st; Thou from the first
Wast present, and with mighty wings outspread
Dove-like satst brooding on the vast Abyss
And mad'st it pregnant: What in me is dark
Illumin, what is low raise and support;
That to the highth of this great Argument
I may assert Eternal Providence,
And justifie the wayes of God to men.

The emphatic opening phrase startles us into attention. It states the theme
of the poem, although the statement of the theme is not complete until the
end of line 26. The second word echoes the opening of the *Odyssey* ''Ανδρα
μοι 'έννεπε μοῦσα ('Tell me, Muse, of the man . . .', but the word
meaning 'man' comes first in the line) and of the *Aeneid*, *arma virumque cano*
('Arms and the man I sing . . .'), and thus asserts its links with the classical
epic tradition, but his subject is very different from that of either Homer or
Virgil. It is not a particular man who happened to have had interesting
adventures that Milton is making the subject of his poem, but the First Man,
primal man, the man whose disobedience to God's command changed
human destiny. He is, as the poem is to make clear in many different ways, an
all-embracing Man, in whom the fate of all men is bound up. In line 26
Milton uses 'men' not 'man': his poem is to justify the ways of God to those
particular men — a minority, as we shall eventually learn — who constitute
the 'fit audience though few' whom Milton is addressing. He is going to talk
to some selected *men* about the first and all-inclusive *man*. As we read the first
line we feel that there must be some kind of stress on the 'Dis' of
'Disobedience', to contrast the word with 'obedience' and to suggest the
fatefulness of the action. There must be stress, too, on 'First', since in the
Christian view it was this original act of disobedience that produced the
human condition as we know it. The opening four words in fact go
somewhat against the normal stress pattern of Milton's blank verse, and this
shows Milton's daring, as the stress pattern has not yet been established,
though the second line soon establishes it. We are hit by the massive opening
phrase, but we are not allowed to pause there, the line dropping in intensity
with the two little words 'and the' as it runs up to its other great stress, the
word 'Fruit'. But we cannot stop here; the sense is incomplete and we are
urged on; it is 'the Fruit/Of that Forbidden Tree, . . .' At first we think of

'Fruit' as meaning 'consequences': the fruit of Adam's action. This metaphorical sense of the word is not rejected, even though we are led on at once to the literal sense; it is the fruit of the forbidden tree that he is talking about. But that fruit produces itself fruit in the other sense, the sense of consequence, as the poem goes on to tell us. It was the fruit 'whose mortal tast/Brought Death into the World, and all our woe, . . .'

We are not allowed to pause here, even though those three eloquent and elemental monosyllabic words 'all our woe' sing out with mournful appeal to arrest our thoughts and emotions, but the verse moves on to give a part-definition of the woe 'With loss of *Eden*,' and then, with only a comma's pause, we leap forward to the Christian scheme of redemption, 'till one greater Man/Restore us, and regain the blissful Seat, . . .' And then at last the emphatic verb, of which all the proceeding is the object: 'Sing Heav'nly Muse, . . .' Although we have now got a statement of the subject of the poem, we are not yet allowed to pause but are led on in a steady flow of verse to learn about the remarkable nature of the Muse whom Milton is invoking:

> that on the secret top
> Of *Oreb*, or of *Sinai*, didst inspire
> That Shepherd, who first taught the chosen Seed
> In the Beginning how the Heav'ns and Earth
> Rose out of *Chaos*: . . .

Mount Horeb (Milton prefers the Vulgate form Oreb for its sound, though he was well acquainted with the Hebrew Bible and the Hebrew form Horeb) was where Moses was minding the flock of his father-in-law Jethro when the angel of the Lord appeared to him in the flame of the burning bush: it was generally taken to be the same as Mount Sinai where Moses received the Ten Commandments from God. Moses was a literal shepherd before he became the shepherd of the people of Israel; in a sense he was the archetypal shepherd. Milton refers to him as 'That Shepherd' as though to emphasize that his readers know very well whom he is talking about; the phrase embraces his readers and himself in a common tradition. He is appealing for inspiration to the Heavenly Muse who inspired Moses on Horeb or on Sinai — that is the divine inspiration that Moses received at the burning bush, when he was summoned by God to serve his people as leader and prophet, and the divine revelation to him of the Ten Commandments. For Milton (as he made clear in his earlier poem *Lycidas*) the true great poet combined the functions of shepherd, prophet and priest, and in these lines he wants to ring out suggestions of all there. Moses was also the great teacher to whom was attributed the writing of the first five books of the Bible, beginning with Genesis and its opening words 'In the beginning', which Milton introduces at line 9 to remind us of the beginning of the Creation story as told in Genesis.

The phrase 'the secret top' suggests some kind of special mystical communication and illustrates Milton's ability to use simple words in a highly resonant manner. Other suggestions are at work too in these opening lines. We expect the shepherd (in the sense of a pastor) to teach his *flock*, but instead it is 'That shepherd who first taught the chosen *seed*', that is the chosen people of Israel, and the word 'seed' makes connection with the earlier words 'fruit' and 'tree' and with the massive garden imagery of vegetation used both literally and figuratively throughout *Paradise Lost*.

Milton's verse carries us on by ambiguities. Consider again the placing of the phrase 'In the Beginning':

> That Shepherd, who first taught the chosen Seed,
> In the Beginning how the Heav'ns and Earth
> Rose out of *Chaos*: . . .

Is Milton saying that the shepherd taught the chosen seed in the beginning, or that he taught them how in the beginning Heaven and Earth were created out of chaos? At first we think he is saying the former, then we realize it is the latter, then again we realize that both meanings are involved. This is a typical example of how Milton keeps modifying and enriching his meanings by the ways in which he keeps his verse moving.

Milton wishes to seek heavenly inspiration for his 'adventrous Song' in as inclusive a manner as possible. He invokes the Heavenly Muse of Mount Horeb or of Mount Sinai (different aspects of the same divine power) and then goes on — once more without real pause — to offer the Heavenly Muse further alternatives:

> Or if *Sion* Hill
> Delight thee more, and *Siloa*'s Brook that flow'd
> Fast by the Oracle of God; I thence
> Invoke thy aid . . .

Sion (again Milton prefers the Vulgate spelling to the English Bible's *Zion*, which transliterates the Hebrew) was the hill in south-west Jerusalem on which the Temple ('the Oracle of God') was built; near by was '*Siloa*'s Brook', referred to in the Book of Isaiah as 'the waters of Shiloah that go softly' and in the Gospel of John as 'the pool of Siloam' as well as elsewhere in the Bible and taken by later commentators as a symbol of divine healing or of spiritual inspiration. Milton saw it as a divine equivalent of the Greek well Aganippe on Mount Helicon (which is also the '*Aeonian* Mount'), sacred to the nine muses (the 'Sisters of the sacred well' of *Lycidas*). His multiple sources of inspiration, all deriving ultimately from a single divine spirit, are both more numerous and more genuine than the classical ones, as his subject is to be greater and more universal than anything in classical epic:

> my adventrous Song,
> That with no middle flight intends to soar
> Above th' *Aeonian* Mount, while it pursues
> Things unattempted yet in Prose or Rhyme.

It is an extraordinary boast, even though it echoes with deliberate irony Ariosto's similar boast in *Orlando Furioso*. What exactly does it mean? The story of man's fall and later redemption had been told in the Bible; the story of the Creation, which is told in Books VI and VII of *Paradise Lost*, had been told not only in the Book of Genesis, the original source, but in English poetry by Joshua Sylvester's *Divine Weeks and Works*, a version of the French Protestant epic on the Creation by Guillaume de Salluste du Bartas, which Milton certainly knew and from which he got some details. Yet Milton is not simply re-telling the Bible story. His epic fills out in remarkable imaginative detail the whole extraordinary cycle of events from the fall of the rebel angels virtually to the end of human history, concentrating with great psychological intensity on the relationship between Adam and Eve and the circumstances and consequences of their fall. When Milton put words into the mouths of Satan and his colleagues, of Adam and Eve, of God's angels and archangels, and, most daringly, of God himself, he knew that he was *inventing* them. Yet he clearly felt that, with divine inspiration, what he was about to tell was the truth. He knows he is making up details of a story whose outlines alone he gets from Scripture and sometimes not even from there; but he is confident that his is a divinely inspired fiction that is wholly different from classical or medieval or Renaissance epics or romances and thus has a gravity and a relevance lacking in those others.

Even though Milton comes to a temporary pause with the startling line 'Things unattempted yet in Prose or Rhyme', this is not the end of his seeking for sources of inspiration, for he moves on at once with the simple conjunction 'and':

> And chiefly Thou O Spirit, that does prefer
> Before all Temples th' upright heart and pure,
> Instruct me, for Thou know'st; Thou from the first
> Wast present, and with mighty wings outspread
> Dove-like satst brooding on the vast Abyss
> And mad'st it pregnant: What in me is dark
> Illumin, what is low raise and support;
> That to the highth of this great Argument
> I may assert Eternal Providence,
> And justifie the wayes of God to men.

Now at last the opening movement of Book I is concluded. Milton has proceeded with great boldness to address God directly, for it is God who prefers 'th' upright heart and pure'. ('Lord, who shall abide in thy

tabernacle? Who shall dwell in thy holy hill? He that walketh uprightly, and
worketh righteousness, and speaketh the truth in his heart.' Psalm 15.) It is
the creative spirit of God that created the universe itself that he now, in this
climactic passage, invokes. Milton is recalling quite precisely the second verse
of Genesis: 'And the Spirit of God moved upon the face of the waters.' The
line 'Dove-like satst brooding on the vast Abyss' shows Milton's awareness
of all the connotations involved in the Hebrew word *merachepeth* which the
Authorized Version of the Bible translates simply as 'moved' in Genesis 1, 2
but which both Jewish and Christian commentators took to imply brooding
and hatching as a bird broods over and hatches its eggs. So it is clear that
when Milton turns to 'chiefly Thou o Spirit' that he is appealing to the
highest creative source in the divine nature to inspire and sustain him in a
work that is by implication to be as authoritative (because inspired by the
same source) as the words of Moses himself. Even more daringly, creation of
Paradise Lost is implicitly compared to the creation of the world.

Milton is aware of his great daring. We sense the urgency of his appeal in
the rocking motion of the lines 'What in me is dark/Illumin, what is low
raise and support;' before he rises up to a statement of his grand ambition:

> That to the highth of this great Argument
> I may assert Eternal Providence,
> And justifie the wayes of God to men.

Milton the poet, the maker (the Greek *poietes* means 'maker'), appeals to
God the creator and quickener of all things to help him write this unprecedented epic poem. He appeals quite literally for *inspiration*, a 'breathing in',
and the breath or spirit he wishes breathed into him is the *ruach* or spirit of
God. And, boldest claim of all, he is doing it for God's sake. He uses 'assert'
in the sense of 'maintain the cause of, champion, defend' (sense 2 in the
Oxford English Dictionary). His poem will defend and justify God's
behaviour. Is it going too far to say that the implication is that God needs
Milton's help? But of course men need it too, for only if they appreciate
God's justice can they adopt the true religious attitude.

A lot more could be said about the first 26 lines of *Paradise Lost*, and one
could go through the whole poem bringing out the suggestions and implications of the language, listening to the remarkable modulations of the verse as
the lines simultaneously move forward and refer backwards to what they
have already said, exploring the inter-related imagery and the rich patterns of
suggestion it sets up, showing the moments of irony and even of humour,
and above all demonstrating that Milton had not simply one style, a grand
'organ voice', but was master of a great variety of styles each appropriate to
the needs of the poem at a given moment while co-operating in the total

effect. In a study of this scale we can only pick out the more interesting examples.

Before leaving this opening passage, however, let us look briefly at some aspects of its language. It is surprising to see how many words of one syllable Milton employs. This is not only for those conjunctions, relative pronouns and prepositions that link the clauses together as they move, 'and', 'whose', 'with', 'till', 'that', 'who', 'or' and so on. There are also whole lines consisting mostly of monosyllabic words of Anglo-Saxon (as distinct from Latin) origin, such as the line 'Brought Death into the World, and all our woe.' Even line 10 'Rose out of *Chaos*: Or if *Sion* Hill' except for the special words Chaos (Greek) and Sion (Hebrew) consists of simple English monosyllabic words. When Milton introduces words of Latin origin, such as 'Argument' (in the sense of 'subject') and 'Eternal Providence' they are prepared for by the movement of the verse. He announces that he 'intends to soar' 'with no middle flight', and he soars up to lines 23 to 25 with enormous emphasis on 'this great Argument' and 'assert Eternal Providence'. Yet line 26, his daring statement of his motive in writing and the culminating line in the opening of the poem, has only one word of Latin origin, 'justifie'. It is a simple yet eloquent line, and the phrase 'the wayes of God to men' is positively homely beside what could be made of it in Latinate dress (e.g., 'Designs of Deity to Humankind'). Milton shows himself to be what Wordsworth claimed a true poet was, 'a man speaking to men'.

In traditional classical epic style Milton then asks his Muse (in this case the Holy Spirit) to begin to tell the story. 'For Heav'n hides nothing from thy view' asserts the claims of the poetic imagination: the inspired poet can speak of Heaven and 'the deep Tract of Hell' with confidence. Milton is of course aware, and the point is made later in the poem, that events in Heaven and Hell can only be presented to human readers in a way that human understanding can cope with. He is not committed to the literal truth of every detail he presents. Yet in a sense he is, for he feels he is writing with divine inspiration and, further, he makes clear in his *Christian Doctrine* that, even though God in the Bible exhibits Himself to men 'not as He really is, but in such a manner as may be within the scope of our comprehension' yet we must believe God when He reveals in the Bible that God made man in His own image, after His likeness. So if the modern reader finds the excessive anthropomorphism of the scenes in Heaven somewhat distasteful, he cannot altogether explain it away in allegorical or symbolic terms, for Milton clearly believed that God, and much more so angels, were more like men than some Platonic interpreters of the Bible believed or than most modern theologians would allow. The main point, however, is that he trusted his poetic imagination under the divine inspiration he sought and, he believed, obtained.

The first question Milton asks his divine Muse to answer is the most crucial of all both for Milton himself and for Christian theology:

> Say first, for Heav'n hides nothing from thy view
> Nor the deep Tract of Hell, say first what cause
> Mov'd our Grand Parents in that happy State,
> Favour'd of Heav'n so highly, to fall off
> From thir Creator, and transgress his Will
> For one restraint, Lords of the World besides?

The initial answer is sudden and explosive: 'Th' infernal Serpent'. The phrase is spat out in a tone of contempt and horror. Milton, as is to become clear later, is in a bit of a quandary here, because the third chapter of the Book of Genesis attributes the temptation of Eve and the subsequent fall of both her and Adam to the serpent, a creature 'more subtil than any beast of the field which the Lord God had made'. There is no suggestion at all in the Genesis story that the serpent was really Satan or the Devil or anything but a snake, and although later development of the story of the Fall in Christian thought equated the serpent with Satan, the chief of the fallen angels, there is no mention in the Genesis account of Satan or of the fall of the angels (the story of the rebellion and fall of Satan and his fellows is a much later development arising from the interpretation of the line in Isaiah XIV, 12 'How art thou fallen from heaven, O Lucifer, son of the Morning' where Lucifer, meaning 'light bearer', actually refers to Babylon). So Milton, bound by the Genesis story, must in the first instance attribute the fall to 'th' infernal serpent', and gets considerable poetic effect by his placing of that phrase in immediate answer to his question. But he cannot leave it at that; the presentation and characterization of Satan and his crew, embodying as they do the whole range of vices to which man is prone, is an essential part of his story. So he goes on immediately to identify the serpent with the chief of the Rebel Angels who deceived the Mother of Mankind for his own nefarious purposes after he had been cast out of Heaven. Note how in lines 34–6 Milton leans on the words 'guile', 'deceiv'd' and 'Pride' (all coming emphatically at the end of a line) and moves the story on with the phrase 'what time' which takes us immediately into the expulsion of the Rebel Angels from Heaven. The movement of the verse is carried on by 'with', 'by whose aid', 'and':

> he it was, whose guile
> Stird up with Envy and Revenge, deceiv'd
> The Mother of Mankind, what time his Pride
> Had cast him out from Heav'n, with all his Host
> Of Rebel Angels, by whose aid aspiring
> To set himself in Glory above his Peers,
> He trusted to have equal'd the most High,
> If he oppos'd; and with ambitious aim
> Against the Throne and Monarchy of God
> Rais'd impious War in Heav'n and Battel proud
> With vain attempt. Him the Almighty Power
> Hurld headlong flaming from th' Ethereal Skie.

The words 'ambitious', 'impious', 'proud', 'vain' (in both senses) give a sense of fierce moral indignation to the account. The verse then goes on (in the middle of a line) to concentrate on Satan, with a deliberate reversal of the normal word-order ('Him the Almighty Power / Hurld headlong . . .') to pinpoint the villain. After the reference of Satan's ejection down 'To bottomless perdition' the verse turns round, as it were, to remind us again who the ejected character was and why he met this fate in a line which rounds out a striking cadence: 'Who durst defy th' Omnipotent to Arms'.

'Bottomless perdition' works better as a phrase suggestive of utter loss and woe than any attempt to visualize Hell precisely could. Milton goes on to build up an atmosphere of despair and damnation with phrases like 'Confounded though immortal', 'lost happiness', 'huge affliction and dismay', 'dismal Situation waste and wilde', 'sights of woe', 'Regions of sorrow', and the striking line 'No light, but rather darkness visible'. There is no pause as the verse moves on with suggestion after suggestion, and then proceeds to build up a sense of total contrast between 'God and light of Heav'n' and the prison of utter (which means 'outer' as well as 'total') darkness to which the rebel angels are now confined. A line consisting (except for the third word) of monosyllabic words, with every word of simple Anglo-Saxon origin, sums up this contrast: 'O how unlike the place from whence they fell!' Without pause the verse proceeds to move from Satan to his second-in-command:

> . . . and weltering by his side
> One next himself in power, and next in crime,
> Long after known in *Palestine*, and named
> *Beelzebub*.

Beëlzebub (four syllables), 'lord of flies', long held to be the great corrupter of man, is mentioned here in an emphatic position at the beginning of a line and before a pause. The word falls on the ear with a horrid thud, emphasized by the three 'b' sounds. Originally the Philistine sun-god, a manifestation of the great deity Baal, he was believed to have given answers to his worshippers by the motion of the swarms of flies that arose around sacrifices made to him. As so often in his description of the fallen angels, Milton invokes a whole area of suggestions relating to the struggle of the people of Israel against the cruel and vicious practices of the gods of ancient Palestine, through whom the fallen angels sought to wreak their vengence on man and God.

The speeches of Satan and Beelzebub and (in Book II) of Moloch, Belial and Mammon are highly skilled exercises in rhetoric, the art of persuasion, in which the speakers use a dazzling variety of persuasive devices to convince the others of the rightness of their point of view. This splendid verse rhetoric is meant to be evil presenting itself as good, 'making the worse appear the better cause' as Socrates' enemies accused him of doing, and of course it is enormously impressive, both poetically and as argument. If evil could not be made out to be attractive and was readily recognized as nasty there would be no problem for men and leading the good life would be easy and natural. To argue that Milton was unconsciously on Satan's side because he puts such splendidly persuasive poetry into his mouth is naïvely to misconstrue what Milton is doing here. That it *is* evil, however, is clear from a close examination of the arguments presented: the best part of C.S. Lewis's *Preface to Paradise Lost* is the chapter in which he provides this examination and demonstrates the different kinds of evil represented by the different speakers, from the perversion of potential great and good qualities displayed by Satan to the simple fury of Moloch and Mammon's attempt to persuade himself and others that Hell is just as good as Heaven.

The broken cadence of the first line of Satan's address to Beelzebub sounds an elegiac note of loss and sadness:

> If thou beest he; But O how fall'n how chang'd
> From him, who in the happy Realms of Light
> Cloth'd with transcendent brightness didst out-shine
> Myriads though bright: . . .

But Satan goes on to boast of his unchangeable will, his sense of 'high disdain' and of 'injur'd merit' (a strong will can be a virtue, so can disdain if turned to the proper object; a sense of injured merit, however, is a self-indulgent pose, especially in the light of what we are to learn about Satan, whose merit was never injured). The verse moves steadily from the elegiac to the boastful to the defiant:

> What though the field be lost?
> All is not lost; the unconquerable Will,
> The study of revenge, immortal hate,
> And courage never to submit or yield:
> And what is else not to be overcome?

The first two lines ring out with splendid assertion: in a good cause such eloquence would be wholly commendable, but with the phrases 'the study of revenge' and 'immortal hate' we move into a realm of barrenness and negativeness; studied revenge and hate sustained for ever certainly do not represent Christian virtues nor are they virtues on most moral or religious codes. To a Christian, certainly, the courage to repent is more difficult and more admirable than stubbornness in hate. At this point Satan's words begin to sound more impressive than the meaning they actually convey. Nevertheless, resolution and strength of will motivating a continuing fight against hopeless odds are in a way admirable, and at this stage Satan is clearly an impressive figure, as Milton means him to be.

To Beelzebub's reply, questioning the possibility of further action, Satan continues in a style that still has force and dignity but which becomes steadily plainer as the essential nastiness of his proposal becomes clear:

> Fall'n Cherube, to be weak is miserable
> Doing or Suffering: but of this be sure,
> To do ought good never will be our task,
> But ever to do ill our sole delight,
> As being contrary to his high will
> Whom we resist. If then his Providence
> Out of our evil seek to bring forth good,
> Our labour must be to pervert that end,
> And out of good still to find means of evil; . . .

A sinister force falls on the word 'pervert' in line 164.

The interest then shifts to the physical appearance of these great evil characters, lying 'Prone on the Flood, extended long and large'. A sense of wonder takes over, and Milton draws on a variety of classical and biblical legends of monstrous creatures to convey the awed horror with which Satan is to be viewed. Then, characteristically with a minimal pause, Milton modulates the tone again into something both strange and humanly appealing, drawing on the old story of sailors mistaking a whale for an island; he is referring to the great Leviathan, to whom he has compared Satan:

> Him haply slumbring on the *Norway* foam
> The Pilot of some small night-founder'd Skiff,
> Deeming some Island, oft, as Sea-men tell,
> With fixed Anchor in his skaly rind
> Moors by his side under the Lee, while Night
> Invests the Sea, and wished Morn delayes: . . .

'The Pilot of some small night-founder'd Skiff' belongs to the ordinary world of men as we now know them; yet at the same time the idea of a pilot anchoring on a huge sea-monster under the impression that it is an island is extremely bizarre. The pilot is deluded, and so for the moment is the reader. Satan after all is the master of delusion, and in medieval bestiaries where the story of sailors anchoring on whales can be found we sometimes find the treacherous whale referred to as a type of Satan. But Milton's main interest here — one might say his main *poetic* interest — is to find language that moves between the monstrous and the familiar. The evocation of the pilot waiting patiently by what he imagines to be an island 'while Night/Invests the Sea, and wished Morn delays', in spite of a slightly sinister suggestion of stealth and deception, pleases and refreshes with its evocation of darkness and hush — but only for a moment, for we are reminded at once of who is involved: 'So stretcht out huge in length the Arch-fiend lay.'

At this point Milton finds it necessary to remind the reader that Satan, now lying 'Chain'd on the burning Lake', could never have risen again without God's permission, which was granted in order that Satan might damn himself further with repeated crimes and also that he might in the end be enraged to see God bringing good out of evil and then punished with 'treble confusion, wrath and vengeance'. If Milton chooses to bring in here a logical and a theological argument, then the reader has no option but to encounter it as such and he may well feel unsatisfied by the implications. If all Satan's evil machinations against man, with their appalling consequences, could have been prevented by the simple expedient of God's keeping him chained on the burning lake, then it is clear that God (who, Milton held, had total foreknowledge of everything that was to happen) planned the Fall of Man, partly in order to make Satan worthy of even more horrible punishment and partly so that in the end God could bring good out of evil (although the history of the world after the Fall as presented to Adam by Michael in Book XII shows an appalling amount of evil remaining). This problem, of God's responsibility, as a totally all-powerful and all-foreseeing power, for everything that was to happen in His creation is an intractable one. Milton feels the need to come to terms with it head-on if he is to justify the ways of God to men, and he does so more than once in the course of the poem. But in fact the strength and conviction of the poem lie elsewhere. The poetry, as we shall see, has a powerful logic of its own.

When Satan speaks again, no longer chained on the burning lake but upright and mighty in stature, his note is elegiac: 'Farewell happy fields/Where joy forever dwells.' He goes on to welcome Hell, his abode from now, in the best terms possible for him. He will accept its horrors, for in Hell he will still be master of himself bringing with him

> A mind not to be chang'd by Place or Time.
> The mind is its own place, and in it self
> Can make a Heav'n of Hell, a Hell of Heav'n.

This is truer than Satan thinks. The irony is that Satan's mind *does* make its own place, which becomes progressively more dreadful. And since Hell is in his own mind he carries its tortures around with him wherever he goes. We are reminded of the scene in Marlowe's *Doctor Faustus* where Faustus asks Mephistophilis how it is that he is out of Hell and Mephistophilis replies:

> Why that is hel, nor am I out of it:
> Thinkst thou that I who saw the face of God,
> And tasted the eternal joyes of heaven,
> Am not tormented with ten thousand hels,
> In being depriv'd of everlasting blisse?

Milton is enjoying the ironies of the situation in a grimly humorous way. When Satan makes his ringing declaration 'Better to reign in Hell, than serve in Heav'n' it sounds splendidly melodramatic in a a Byronic sort of way, but he has already conceded that there is an appalling difference between 'this mournful gloom' and the 'celestial light' of Heaven, and that Heaven possesses the 'happy Fields/Where Joy for ever dwells' while Hell has 'horrours', so the word 'better' in this line is really empty. All Satan is really saying is that so long as he is boss he doesn't give a damn (in the most literal sense) what he is boss of. This public rhetoric of Satan's certainly has its appeal, but read carefully in its context it is seen as a combination of vanity, self-deception, whistling in the dark and rabble-rousing.

Milton soon shifts the perspective again and in lines 283 and following we see Satan, in full armour, moving towards the shore. His shield and spear (following classical epic precedent) are described through elaborate similes which bring the ordinary world of Milton's day into the poem, and then we turn and see his massed legions 'Thick as Autumnial Leaves that strow the Brooks/*In Vallombrosa*', where Milton draws on the memory of his Italian journey (when he visited Vallombrosa from nearby Florence) in 1638 and in doing so both reduces the scale of the fallen angels, from monsters to fallen leaves, indicates their huge numbers, and associates them with barrenness and death (these are *dead* leaves, and in any case fallen leaves had been since Homer a symbol of the numberless dead). The personal memory and the precise location of the landscape give a special touch of freshness to the gloomy picture; and then Milton shifts his perspective again and goes on to compare the fallen angels to Pharaoh's horsemen drowned in the attempt to cross the Red Sea:

> Afloat, when with fierce Winds *Orion* arm'd
> Hath vext the Red-Sea Coast, whose waves orethrew
> *Busiris* and his *Memphian* Chivalry,
> While with perfidious hatred they pursu'd
> The Sojourners of *Goshen*, who beheld
> From the safe shore thir floating Carkasses
> And broken Chariot Wheels, so thick bestrown
> Abject and lost lay these, covering the Flood,
> Under amazement of thir hideous change.

Note how Milton winds the verse along, with 'when', 'whose', 'while', moving from a comparison of the fallen angels to the scattered sedge afloat on the Red Sea (and Milton knew that the Hebrew words for Red Sea, '*yam suph*', meant sea of reeds, or *reed* sea) to a reminder that Pharaoh's host, similar in numbers and attitude to the fallen angels, had been overthrown there. Milton, with the best scholarship of his day, erroneously identified the biblical Pharaoh with Busiris, but in any case he needed the sound of that line 'Busiris and his *Memphian* Chivalry', with 'Busiris' suggesting what he called in his *Nativity Ode* 'the brutish gods of Egypt' '*Isis* and *Orus* and the Dog

Anubis'. 'Memphian' is simply 'Egyptian', from the Egyptian city of
Memphis, but it is *'Memphian* Chivalry' because Milton wanted to associate
Pharaoh's host with the chivalric hosts of medieval romance: the vanity of
medieval romance and the ethical superiority of his epic to stories of knights
and fair ladies is a Miltonic belief that emerges more than once in *Paradise
Lost*.

Satan summons his followers, scattered like autumn leaves, with a clarion
call that echoes throughout the depths of Hell, venting a grim humour in his
attempt to rally them:

> Have ye chos'n this place
> After the toyl of Battel to repose
> Your wearied vertue, for the ease you find
> To slumber here, as in the Vales of Heav'n
> Or in this abject posture have ye sworn
> To adore the Conquerour?

He concludes his appeal with the great cry 'Awake, arise, or be for ever
fall'n.' There is another irony here, all unconscious on Satan's part, for in
fact they *are* for ever fallen and they rise only in order to complete the work of
their damnation.

The imagery then speeds on. The host of fallen angels are compared to the
horde of locusts called up by Moses as one of the 10 plagues of Egypt, or they
are a well-disciplined army obeying the signal of 'thir great Sultan'
(overtones here of oriental despotism and cruelty), or, in an image that
invokes with extraordinary power a sense of the barbarians pouring down
from the frozen north to threaten the sunny Mediterranean culture of ancient
Rome, they are

> A multitude, like which the populour North
> Pour'd never from her frozen loyns, to pass
> *Rhene* or the *Danaw*, when her barbarous Sons
> Came like a Deluge on the South, and spread
> Beneath *Gibraltar* to the *Lybian* sands.

Finally, in a long and evocative passage, they are first described as the false
gods who of old tempted the people of Israel and Judah into transgression
and who were to become permanent threats to men, seducing, trapping,
misleading, perverting them into monstrous cruelties and unspeakable
horrors. '*Moloch*, horrid King, besmear'd with blood/Of human sacrifice,
and parents tears' leads the grim procession. A whole history of European
folklore and mythology develops, Semitic, Egyptian, Greek, Roman and
Celtic, each group with its own area of suggestiveness, each presented with
its own historical and human tone, until we almost feel that we have been
presented with a history of the human imagination. And yet it is a roll-call of
evil. We sense all kinds of reservations, many degrees of human interest and

even sympathy, in this rich presentation, Milton being unable to conceal totally his sympathy with some areas at least of pagan mythology – he was a Humanist as well as a Christian, in spite of the fact that in his later career the humanistic element in his thought tended to fade (it should perhaps be made clear at this point that the word 'Humanist' is used throughout this book in its Renaissance sense of someone concerned to rediscover and preserve the best of ancient Greek and Latin literary and philosophical culture). We sense this sympathy most, perhaps, when Milton goes on to describe the fallen angels after they have rallied:

> Anon they move
> In perfect *Phalanx* to the Dorian mood
> Of Flutes and soft Recorders; such as rais'd
> To hight of noblest temper Hero's old
> Arming to Battel, and in stead of rage
> Deliberate valour breath'd, firm and unmov'd . . .

These were fallen angels, beginning their long history of evil plotting against God and man, but they were fallen *angels*, and at this point in their descent still retain some of the graces of their former state. Whether Milton is suggesting that some kinds of artistic activity are only possible after the Fall, and this is an oblique and even unconscious argument in favour of God's allowing it to happen, is more dubious, but this is the *kind* of overtone we find in later parts of *Paradise Lost* when it becomes clear that certain kinds of active virtue are only possible in struggle against evil in a fallen world. Milton will later show us the heavenly hymning of God by the angels in Heaven as well as the simple praise of God by still unfallen man, but the arts of music and literature are far more diverse and rich than this, as Milton well knew; perhaps the Fall was necessary in the interest of the arts. (Or perhaps the arts were necessary to help compensate for the Fall.) The Savage in Aldous Huxley's novel *Brave New World* could not tolerate the world of perfect adjustment and frictionless adaptation to environment to which he was introduced, and wanted to return to the world of danger, difficulty, challenge and tragedy.

To return, however, to the fallen angels, who both 'move in perfect Phalanx' and remain 'firm and unmov'd' in mind – the paradox is part of the careful balancing of the verse that characterizes this passage, with the chiming of similar vowels at the end of lines, 'move', 'mood', 'unmov'd', 'rais'd' and 'rage'. Satan swells with pride as he watches his disciplined host, who are now described in a rich series of similes bringing in both classical mythology and medieval *chansons de geste* and romance. The evocation of the Arthurian story and of the *Chanson de Roland*, together with echoes from Ariosto's *Orlando Furioso* culminates with the lines

When Charlemain with all his peerage fell
By *Fontarabbia*.

It was in fact Roland and not Charlemagne who fell at Roncevalles: Milton changes both the identity of the slain hero and the name of the place of the fatal battle: Fontarabbia is 40 miles from Roncevalles. But Milton wanted the suggestion of Christian and Arab confronting each other, the first Holy Roman Emperor and all his peerage against the Arab civilization that threatened all he stood for. The sustained and complex series of similes thus ends on an elegiac note, with a brief but vivid picture of the forces of Christianity overcome by the infidel. Yet there is another dimension: it is the host of fallen angels, forces of evil, who are compared with the heroes of these romances and heroic tales. The medieval stories in which they figure are for Milton not on the side of truth and virtue. Again and again in *Paradise Lost* the suggestion is made that tales of chivalry are idle; that chivalry will not save; the knightly code and courtly love have superficial attractions but fundamentally they are on the Devil's side. In two lines just before the reference to Charlemagne there is a mention of 'all who since, Baptiz'd or Infidel/Jousted in *Aspramont* or *Montalban*', the second of which used to be hailed by critics as a marvellous evocation of romantic story. But in fact the suggestion is that the fancy goings-on of chivalry are common to Christian and pagan and represent something unserious, rituals of decadence. In some senses, as repeated suggestions throughout the poem indicate, *Paradise Lost* is not only a counter-epic, written within the epic tradition but against it, but a counter-statement aimed at all the traditions of secular poetry of love and war produced by western civilization. There was of course a strong Christian element in the Charlemagne stories and the Arthurian stories, among others, but this was not enough for Milton. The true Christian poet had to engage with reality more seriously. He had long been attracted to these earlier traditions and, as we have seen, once meditated an epic centred on King Arthur: *Paradise Lost* makes clear why he changed his mind.

But we must not exaggerate Milton's repudiation of older epic and romance. Much of it he still found enchanting, as is made clear by the way he lingers over the imagery evoking it. There is an appeal in those stories and those actions and those codes of honour, and if they are associated at this point in his poem with the fallen angels this is partly because evil has its plausible and attractive side and partly because life as we apprehend it – as man apprehends it after the Fall – consists of a curiously mingled yarn of good and evil and any forms of expression available to a poet must avail themselves of this mingling. Milton is describing a conclave of fallen angels; later in the poem he describes events in Heaven and in the Garden of Eden before the Fall. All he has at his disposal is experience of a fallen world, so all his language, all his illustrations, all his imagery, must come from this experience. There is a further and subtler point that emerges by the time the poem reaches its conclusion: it concerns the ambiguity of both good and evil and ways in which one may become the other.

Satan in a further speech announces his plans to 'pry' into the rumoured creation of man by God and ends with a passionate declaration of war against God which is hailed by brandished swords and clashing of arms on shields by the assembled host. The imagery here is suggestive of one of the great rallies that Hitler used to stage at Nuremberg: we almost expect to hear the shouts of 'Sieg Heil!' We might ask, incidentally, what are swords and shields doing in this context? Angels, even when fallen, are immortal, and the instruments of death-dealing and protection from death-dealing appropriate to men seem fatuous when associated with these creatures. The question raises itself much more insistently in Raphael's account of the war in Heaven. Milton tries to justify his use of the paraphernalia of human combat, explaining that though angels cannot be killed they can be temporarily wounded, and so on. But all this is surely shadow boxing. God, all-powerful, all-knowing, all-foreknowing, does not need to have His supporters fight it out with arms and armour against the rebels against His power. As act of will on His part could bring about instantaneously what He wants to happen (and knows will happen, for He has a total foreknowledge), as Milton makes clear at other points in the poem. Some recent critics have seen the war in Heaven as the central part of Milton's epic; it may seem so on a purely formal reading of the poem, but in terms of the cumulative meaning achieved by the poem as it moves towards its conclusion it seems rather pointless.

The fallen angels proceed to build their palace of Pandemonium, led on by Mammon, 'the least erected Spirit that fell/From heav'n'. Even before the Fall, Milton goes on to inform us, Mammon had kept his eyes bent on the ground, admiring 'The riches of Heav'ns pavement'. Was he then a defective angel even before he was seduced by Satan into rebellion? Was he created like that? If so that was God's fault. Did he become like that through a misuse of free-will? But even the exercise of free-will would be but expressing the nature with which God endowed him at his creation. Milton does not explore the point, but the alert reader watching to see exactly how Milton is to achieve his aim of justifying the ways of God to men will be given pause.

Pandemonium was designed by the fallen angel who was to become the god called by the Greeks Hephaestus and by the Romans Vulcan or, less commonly, Mulciber. Milton saw the Greek myth of the throwing out from Heaven of Hephaestus by Zeus as an echo of the fall of Satan and his fellow rebel angels. But the appeal of the Greek myth is real, as Milton implicitly acknowledges by the way he changes the whole tone of his narrative to project the reader into a fabled summer eve in the ancient Greek world:

and in *Ausonian* land
Men call'd him *Mulciber*; and how he fell
From Heav'n, they fabl'd, thrown by angry *Jove*

> Sheer o're the Chrystal Battlements; from Morn
> To Noon he fell, from Noon to dewy Eve,
> A Summers day; and with the setting Sun
> Dropt from the Zenith like a falling Star,
> On *Lemnos* th' *Aegaean* Ile: . . .

At first we are watching from the battlements as Mulciber is thrown over, and we see him falling, falling, down through immense space, a whole summer's day: but with the phrase 'A Summers day' we are on earth in summer time; the perspective changes, and we now see the falling god dropping out of the sky as we look up from Lemnos. It is a picture of charm rather than of horror, as though Greek mythology could make acceptable the terrible story of the fall of the rebel angels. But Milton hastens on to tell us that the Greek version is not true:

> thus they relate,
> Erring; for he with this rebellious rout
> Fell long before; nor aught avail'd him now
> To have built in Heav'n high Towrs; . . .

'Rebellious rout' restores the note of moral disgust, and the quiet incisiveness of 'nor aught avail'd him now/To have built in Heav'n high Towrs' provides a note of contemptuous dismissal.

Book I ends with the reduction of the fallen angels to pygmy size to accommodate them all in Pandemonium (but the reduction in size also reduces their impressiveness and helps to make their plottings sound mean and silly). In an inner chamber the leaders 'in their own dimensions' 'In close recess and secret conclave sat.' The word 'conclave' to seventeenth-century English Protestants suggested Jesuit plottings, which were regarded as both nefarious and treasonable. And so 'the great consult began'.

Book II

The first part of Book II is a report of 'the great consult', ending with the decision to avoid open war and investigate the possibilities of corrupting God's new creation, man. It opens with a vivid picture of conspicuous power, where Satan sits in oriental luxury on a gem-studded throne: the images suggest a barbaric despotism with echoes of Israelite suspicions of the civilizations of Babylon and Egypt and, more specifically, ancient Greek and Roman suspicions of the rich and despotic Persians. The speeches that follow show Milton deploying his remarkable rhetorical skills in giving persuasive plausibility to arguments in which each speaker reveals a different kind and degree of moral evil. Satan's opening speech, though magnificent in its rhetoric, is riddled with contradictions and nonsense. He asserts that he is the Leader 'through just right, and the fit Laws of Heav'n' and also by his followers' 'free choice'; that nonetheless nobody will bother about precedence in Hell since that simply means more pain; that this fact is conducive 'to union, and firm Faith, and firm accord' greater than could be achieved in Heaven; and that with this unprecedented faith and accord they 'now return/To claim our just inheritance of old'. He is followed by Moloch, 'the simplest of the fiends; a mere rat in a trap', says C.S. Lewis, but there is more to him than that, for we are told that he had a passionate ambition to be 'deem'd equal in strength' with God, that that ambition dissipated all his fear, and that he would rather not exist at all than fail to achieve it. A rat in a trap is not characterized by self-destructive ambition. And there is a perversion of a noble ideal here in committing oneself to make a total sacrifice for something one aims at. He advises open war; whatever the consequences, nothing could be worse than to continue 'to dwell here, driv'n out from bliss'; they will force their 'resistless way' back into Heaven; yet it turns out that they will not be 'resistless' for Heaven is 'inaccessible', so the best they can do is to annoy God with 'perpetual inroads' 'Which if not Victory, is yet Revenge.' As so often with the speech of the fallen angels, the logic deteriorates as the speech develops, and the final counsel of despair, to seek revenge rather than victory, is a hollow declaration.

Belial follows, with a speech full of questions and answers (both supplied by himself) and an air of carefully reasoned deliberation. His conclusion is that they should make the best of a bad job and learn how to acclimatize themselves to Hell. It is interesting that Milton does not approve of Belial's advice not to resist God further: 'Thus *Belial* with words cloath'd in reasons garb/Counsel'd ignoble ease and peaceful sloth'. Is it then better to fight for what you want, even if what you want is evil? Once again, we see some of the moral ambiguities with which the poem is shot through. Belial had been described earlier as 'in act more graceful and humane' than Moloch, and Milton added 'A fairer person lost not Heav'n'.

Mammon follows, advising his fellows to come to terms with their present situation, which indeed has its own advantages and can in fact be regarded as comparable to Heaven. Thus he agrees with Belial in counselling peace, and the assembly approve this advice. Satan is taken aback that the debate is going the wrong way, so he puts up Beelzebub to suggest a new idea, that is to substitute 'Some easier enterprize' for open war. Instead of attacking God directly, they could attack him through his new creation man. Emphasizing that although the proposal was Beelzebub's it was originally devised by Satan, Milton stresses the horror of this 'devilish Counsel', reflecting

> So deep a malice, to confound the race
> Of mankind in one root, and Earth with Hell
> To mingle and involve, . . .

Why did God allow this plan to proceed and to be successful? As though

Milton is aware of the question at this point, he drops in a parenthetical 'But thir spite still serves/His glory to augment.' But it is not God's glory that is at issue: it is His responsibility for man's suffering.

Satan has got the result he wanted, and with concealed irony congratulates the assembly on their good judgment. He then asks who is going to explore the 'dark unbottom'd infinite Abyss' to find the newly created world where the even more newly created man is to be found. Nobody offers himself for this dangerous venture (this is a deliberate contrast with the later debate in Heaven, where Christ offers himself to suffer for man) and Satan announces that he will go. He vaingloriously describes the dangers he is prepared to encounter to seek 'Deliverance for us all'. This is of course the nonsense rhetoric of a cunning demagogue. In no possible way could Satan's successful contrivance of the Fall of Man produce deliverance for him and his colleagues; it would be an act of pure spite, and all parties would be worse off. But this is the demagogic rhetoric of public policy, and it is not unknown in our own time.

The debate over, the assembly disperses to engage in a variety of occupations, which are described with sad sympathy as the occupations with which fallen man attempts to console, entertain or enlighten himself. They celebrate their deeds in ravishing heroic song, or debate the great philosophical questions (but 'found no end, in wand'ring mazes lost' – because they had lost the key to truth) or engage in geographical exploration. These are all activities dear to Milton, and though they are shown as vain they are also shown as attractive, except for the explorers, who are after all exploring the geography of Hell, in describing which Milton effectively draws on a variety of classical and other myths. Hell is in fact whatever the human imagination throughout the whole of history has conceived it to be. Those who explore the confines of their new territory found everything that symbolized perpetual unfulfilled search, unending grief, eternal deprivation of light and grace and satisfying rational meaning.

The reader is trapped in the adjectives; 'forlorn', 'shuddring horror pale' (a characteristic Miltonic order, here most effectively used), 'agast', 'lamentable', 'dark and drearier', 'dolorous', and others, give a nightmare sense of exhausting every possible avenue of escape. The three woeful adjectives 'abominable, inutterable, and worse' complement the line of monosyllabic nouns, 'Rooks, Caves, Fens, Bogs, Dens, and shades of death'. Criticism of Milton for not being specific enough in his imagery here and elsewhere is surely misguided. What is wanted in this context, and what Milton provides superbly, is richly reverberating suggestions of all that the human imagination has most recoiled from.

Satan's journey through Chaos and his encounter with Sin and Death, which take up the remainder of Book II, are presented through a strange and powerful amalgam of incidents, images and situations partly allegorical, partly symbolic, partly suggestive. As so often, classical and biblical sources mingle, as in the account of the birth of Sin, who in turn brought forth Death. Sin, 'the Portress of Hell Gate', unlocks the gate (Milton does not explain why God allows this, though he makes clear that He has forbidden Sin to do so) and Satan emerges into Chaos,

> a dark
> Illimitable Ocean without bound,
> Without dimension, where length, breadth & highth,
> And time and place are lost; . . .

Chaos is presided over by an 'umpire' also called Chaos, but his is a chaotic presidency:

> *Chaos* Umpire sits,
> And by decision more embroils the fray
> By which he reigns: next him high Arbiter
> *Chance* governs all.

Chaos is presumably not the result of the fall of the rebel angels; it has existed from the beginning of time, as 'the Womb of nature and perhaps her Grave', a mass of confused primal matter available to God as 'dark materials to create more Worlds' should He so ordain. Chaos's consort is 'Sable-vested Night, eldest of things'

> and by them stood
> *Orcus* and *Ades*, and the dreaded name
> Of *Demogorgon*; *Rumor* next and *Chance*,
> And *Tumult* and *Confusion* all imbroil'd,
> And *Discord* with a thousand various mouths.

When and why did the all-good and all-powerful God create these? If their existence is not a consequence of the Fall — and it is made clear that it is not — what are they doing in a Christian view of the universe? And what is the place of Chance in a universe governed by almighty God? Chance in fact is responsible for Satan's successful and fateful journey out of Hell, since at one point in his flight he meets 'a vast vacuitie' in which his wings cannot function and would have dropped down 'Ten thousand fadom deep' and gone on falling for ever

> had not by ill chance
> The strong rebuff of som tumultuous cloud
> Instinct with Fire and Nitre hurried him
> As many miles aloft: . . .

If Satan really became free to tempt man 'by ill chance' then in some sense the Fall of Man was just bad luck. Milton seems in this and similar passages in this part of Book II to be carried away by images of disorder, chance, confusion, and a general sense of uncreatedness, as it were, to the point where he evokes kinds of existence that are difficult to reconcile with his over-all scheme. He was clearly thinking of the second verse of Genesis I, 'And the earth was without form and void; and darkness was upon the face of the deep' – the state of affairs immediately before the Creation. The two Hebrew words translated as 'without form and void' are *tohu va-vohu*, and there is a long tradition in both Jewish and Christian thought of providing strange mystical explanations of what the phrase really meant. Milton was aware of this, but he was also thinking of classical and other myths and stories and one has the impression that at this point in *Paradise Lost* he was enjoying building up an atmosphere rather than paying close attention to the logical and theological scheme ostensibly underlying the poem.

One could of course argue that it would be a mistake to inquire too liter-ally into the meaning of the characters of Chaos, Night and the inhabitants of 'the wasteful Deep' since they are part of the general atmosphere of disorder and confusion that is appropriate both to Satan's moral state and to the uncreated region between Hell and Heaven – the created universe was thought of as suspended from Heaven over Chaos, with Hell far below. Satan endures this dangerous adventure in order to seek out the recently created earth and its newest inhabitant, man. In doing so, he paves the way for Sin and Death to follow him ('such was the will of Heav'n', Milton curtly comments, refusing to argue the matter further at this point).

Book II ends with Satan coming up through Chaos to see the pendent world (that is, the earth circled by the seven planetary spheres, one sphere of fixed stars, the crystalline sphere and the outer *primum mobile*), and above it, barely glimpsed, his lost Heaven

> extended wide
> In circuit, undetermind square or round,
> With Opal Towrs and Battlements adorn'd
> Of living Saphire, once his native Seat; . . .

Milton knows better than to attempt to give a precise picture of the shape and structure of Heaven. 'Fast by' Heaven, 'hanging in a golden Chain', he sees the earth. It is ominous that we first see the earth through Satan's eyes. The book ends on a note of dark foreboding: 'Thither full fraught with mischievous revenge,/Accurst, and in a cursed hour he hies.'

Book III
In opening Book III with an eloquent and moving invocation to Light Milton was giving notice of a shift in scene from Hell to Heaven. He is now entering on the most daring part of his epic, the portrayal of God himself and His angels. The divine nature of light, in some ways an embodiment or a symbol of God and Truth, had been the subject of much discussion among

Neo-Platonists and others, and the area of suggestion and reference in these lines is far richer than the modern reader is likely to apprehend without a learned commentary. The whole opening passage is rich in philosophical, theological and personal suggestions. The blind Milton, deprived of physical light, was confident that he had a divine inner light to guide him; he was confident, too, that he would be placed among the great blind poets and prophets of old. There is a brief note of personal elegy in lines 22–4, which shows the deep commitment Milton felt on entering this most ambitious part of the poem.

> Hail, holy Light, offspring of Heav'n first-born,
>   Or of th' Eternal Coeternal beam
> May I express thee unblam'd? since God is light,
> And never but in unapproached light
> Dwelt from Eternitie; dwelt then in thee,
> Bright effluence of bright essence increate.
> Or hear'st thou rather pure Ethereal stream,
> Whose Fountain who shall tell? before the Sun,
> Before the Heavens thou wert, and at the voice
> Of God, as with a Mantle didst invest
> The rising world of waters dark and deep,
> Won from the void and formless infinite.
> Thee I re-visit now with bolder wing,
> Escap't the *Stygian* Pool, though long detain'd
> In that obscure sojourn, while in my flight
> Through utter and through middle darkness borne
> With other notes then to th' *Orphean* Lyre
> I sung of *Chaos* and *Eternal Night*,
> Taught by the heav'nly Muse to venture down
> The dark descent, and up to reascend,
> Though hard and rare: thee I re-visit safe,
> And feel thy sovran vital Lamp; but thou
> Revisit'st not these eyes, that rowle in vain
> To find thy piercing ray, and find no dawn;
> So thick a drop serene hath quencht thir Orbs,
> Or dim suffusion veild. Yet not the more
> Cease I to wander where the Muses haunt
> Cleer Spring, or shadie Grove, or Sunnie Hill,
> Smit with the love of sacred Song; but chief
> Thee *Sion* and the flowrie Brooks beneath
> That wash thy hallowd feet, and warbling flow,
> Nightly I visit: nor somtimes forget
> Those other two equal'd with them in Fate,
> So were I equal'd with them in renown,
> Blind *Thamyris* and blind *Maeonides*,
> And *Tiresias* and *Phineus* Prophets old.

Milton goes on to complain that the satisfying movement of the seasons is invisible to him. This is a most significant passage, for the seasons themselves were part of the curse imposed after the Fall: in prelapsarian Eden there was perpetual spring. But the round of the seasons is to Milton something splendid and moving, as is the agricultural activity (also a consequence of the Fall) associated with it.

> Thus with the Year
> Seasons return, but not to me returns
> Day, or the sweet approach of Ev'n or Morn,
> Or sight of vernal bloom, or Summers Rose,
> Or flocks, or heards, or human face divine;
> But cloud in stead, and ever-during dark
> Surrounds me, from the chearful wayes of men
> Cut off, . . .

The implication is that, in spite of the gloomy picture of the fate of man after the Fall given later in the poem, Milton took satisfaction in its consequences, in seasonal change, in the life of shepherds working in the midst of fallen Nature, in fallen man himself, whose ways are in spite of everything cheerful, while, with deliberate paradox, the human face is the 'human face divine', Godlike in spite of man's fatal lapse. His picture of the seasons reminds us of that eloquent passage in Genesis in which God promises Noah after the flood that never again will He bring a flood upon earth, and the round of the seasons will go on: 'While the earth remaineth, seed-time and harvest, and cold and heat, and summer and winter, and day and night shall not cease.' (This is a passage that Milton refers to twice in his poem, in Book IV, lines 151–2, and in Book XI, lines 896–900.) Once again we have to distinguish the underlying poetic theme of *Paradise Lost* from its overt logical and theological argument. On the theological surface, Milton justifies the ways of God to men by arguing that Adam and Eve abused the free-will with which they were endowed and so deserved a much worse punishment than they in fact received, while the Christian scheme of redemption showed God bringing good out of evil. At the deeper poetic level the poem suggests that the Fall was necessary, not because of the *felix culpa* which enabled God to bring good out of evil, but because only in conditions of change and struggle could there emerge any kind of human virtue in which Milton could really believe.

We move to God looking down from his high throne (flanked by the Son) on Adam and Eve in the Garden of Eden. The generalized language in which the unfallen condition of the first man and woman is described is wholly appropriate to the occasion. The phrase 'the happie Garden' had a grand archetypal ring, resounding with a suggestion of all man's dreams of ideal gardens and ideal happiness. An abstract phrase such as 'immortal fruits of 'joy and love' suggest the inexpressibility in any specific terms known to fallen man of a state that existed before the Fall. They are living in the happy garden in love, yet in 'solitude' — 'blissful solitude' it is true, yet solitude. There is a paradox here that clearly meant much to Milton; it is related to the similar paradox in the concluding lines of the poem, which portray Adam and Eve, now fallen, leaving the once happy garden for ever: 'They hand in hand with wandring steps and slow,/Through *Eden* took thir solitary way.' They were hand in hand yet solitary. Love can produce its own kind of loneliness.

God's speech to the Son, which follows, is less successful; Milton is in considerable degree versifying arguments he used in his *Christian Doctrine* about the compatibility of God's foreknowledge with man's freedom. 'God in his wisdom,' wrote Milton in *Christian Doctrine*, 'determined to create men and angels reasonable beings, and therefore free agents; at the same time he foresaw which way the bias of their will would incline, in the exercise of their own uncontrolled liberty. What then? Shall we say that this foresight or foreknowledge on the part of God imposed on them the necessity of acting in any definite way? No more than if the future event had been foreseen by any human being. . . . Thus Elisha foresaw how much evil Hazael would bring upon the children of Israel in the course of a few years in 2 Kings VIII,12. Yet no one would affirm that the evil took place necessarily on account of foreknowledge of Elisha; for had he never foreknown it, the event would have occurred with equal certainty, through the free will of the agent.' But Elisha did not create Hazael, and God created man, and if man had a particular bias of will then that is the way God made him. Milton in fact gives the argument away in *Paradise Regained* where God tells Gabriel that Satan

> now shall know I can produce a man
> Of female Seed, far abler to resist
> All his sollicitations, . . .

That is Christ, Man Mark II as it were, made with a stronger will than Adam's was. Christ is 'the second Adam' and can show what the improved model can do.

Milton makes a clear distinction between the delusive rhetoric of the speeches of Satan and his followers and the calm, magisterial logic of God's speeches. By this time Milton was suspicious of rhetoric, regarding it as Plato regarded it, as a suspect art of making the irrational appear plausible. For Aristotle, rhetoric was a neutral skill, the art of persuasion that could be applied to good or bad causes. To Cicero and Quintilian in Roman times rhetoric was the desirable art of public debate, appropriate to a good citizen. Milton in the course of his career seems to have moved steadily away from the Ciceronian view through the Aristotelian to the Platonic. In *Paradise*

Regained the rhetoric is exclusively on Satan's side, while Christ's speech is quiet, simple and even bare. The problem, however, with God's speeches in Book III of *Paradise Lost* is that, artfully versified though they are, their appeal is strictly logical, and the reader is therefore forced to make a logical response. The whole argument urged by God, in surprisingly defensive tones, about man's free-will in spite of the foreknowledge and omnipotence of God, his maker, and man's consequent responsibility for his actions and his deserving appalling punishment for his fault, is as an argument open to too many logical objections. And when God goes on to urge that all Adam's posterity justly deserve 'destruction' because of Adam's sin and that he and his descendants all must die 'or Justice must'

> unless for him
> Som other able, and as willing, pay
> The rigid satisfaction, death for death,

the notion that Justice will be satisfied if someone other than the guilty party suffers death — it doesn't matter who it is, so long as someone is killed — is a very bizarre version of the Christian doctrine of vicarious atonement. If either man must die or Justice must die, unless somebody or other, guilty or innocent, suffers death, one is left wondering about the nature of Justice. Is Justice above God, constraining him to unnatural acts?

But of course God's announcement gives Milton the opportunity to introduce the Son with his offer of self-sacrifice and to show in the differing cadence of his speech, with its musical repetitions and gently eloquent inversions, the difference between the discussion in Heaven and the debate in Hell. (But even here the voice of logic can be raised, pointing out that Christ knows very well that he will not really die, that he will 'rise victorious' and triumph over Hell.) The parallels and contrasts between hellish and heavenly debate are most carefully worked out, and part of the complex design of the poem, where the three theatres of action — Heaven, Earth and Hell — are counterpointed in a variety of artful ways.

The other problem, both here and in the account of the war in Heaven, lies in the dubious nature of purposive action when taken by a power who foreknows and in fact foreordained the conclusion. God decided to create man to fill the vacant place of the fallen angels, hoping that in time a sinless human race would rise to live eternally in Heaven. But even before God made this decision he knew — and we are shown him telling the angels — that man would be tempted and would fall, and so the plan would not work, at least not in the way apparently intended originally.

The Son's offer to become man and suffer man's punishment for him — 'Be thou in *Adams* room' is how God sums it up — is followed by his exaltation and celebration. The hailing of the Son by the angelic host makes it clear that in a purely formal sense — but only in a purely formal sense — he is the hero of the poem. By voluntarily offering himself to be in Adam's room he enables God, in some degree at least, to bring good out of evil. Yet he plays far too small a part in *Paradise Lost* to be the real hero. One must distinguish, as so often, between the overt intention and the underlying poetic meaning. One might say that outwardly Christ is the hero and Adam merely the object of conflict — the Troy of the epic, as it were. In the end, however, in terms of the poem as it realizes itself poetically, Adam is the hero; his and Eve's recovery and their going out in the end to face an uncertain and testing future constitute the poem's final heroic act.

When in the latter part of Book III Milton turns from the heavenly scene to show Satan making his way towards the Garden of Eden, the verse at once picks up in liveliness and complexity. Metaphor and simile leap into life, and all the known, tarnished world of fallen man is pressed into service to give richness and moral implication to Satan's behaviour. Satan lands on the sun, and from there contemplates the universe; there, too, he meets Uriel, whom he questions about the direction of Adam's abode, having first disguised himself as 'a stripling Cherube'. The priggish way in which he informs Uriel that he wants to find Adam's home in order to admire God's work and find a further reason for praising Him is matched by the tone of Uriel's reply, which is rather like that of a headmaster speaking to a boy who has asked for extra homework:

> Faire Angel, thy desire which tends to know
> The works of God, thereby to glorifie
> The great Work-Maister, leads to no excess
> That reaches blame, but rather merits praise . . .

It is hard to believe that Milton was not conscious of the note almost of parody here. There is indeed a grimly ironical humour in the passage, for the stripling cherub is really Satan, whom Uriel cannot detect

> For neither Man nor Angel can discern
> Hypocrisie, the onely evil that walks
> Invisible, except to God alone,
> By his permissive will, through Heav'n and Earth: . . .

What about Eve, then, whom we are later shown fooled by Satan's hypocrisy into believing that the snake that spoke to her was a real, genuine snake and not Satan in disguise? When, in *Paradise Regained*, Milton shows us Christ being tempted by Satan in the wilderness it is made absolutely clear that he knows precisely who Satan is. But poor Eve did not know; she was in the same position as Uriel, who gave away top secret information to the great enemy of God and man because he did not know whom he was really speaking to. Yet Uriel is not held guilty by God or Milton, while Eve, 'our credulous Mother', is.

The unsuspecting Uriel points out Paradise to the disguised Satan, and it is significant that we should first see Paradise through Satan's eyes: 'That spot to which I point is *Paradise*, / *Adams* abode, those loftie shades his Bowre.' The splendid emphatic quality of this simple demonstrative statement focuses both on the gesture of the pointer and on the vision of the beholder to whom he is pointing out the scene. It is the second reference to the Garden of Eden (or Paradise) so far; the first is simply to 'the happie Garden', equally forceful in its elemental generality. In Book IV Milton brings us nearer and nearer to Eden, still looking through Satan's eyes, until at last we are close enough to look into the garden and see Adam and Eve in all their primal dignity.

Book IV

Book IV opens with a powerful expression of the impotent wish that an effective warning voice could have been heard by Adam and Eve at this stage (they were in fact warned by Raphael later) telling them of Satan's approach. It is the measure of Milton's frustration in contemplating Satan's progressively successful moves. The catastrophe towards which the poem is inexorably moving is, in Milton's and the general Christian view, the greatest and most central catastrophe of all human history and determined the nature of life on earth for all humankind. It was all foreseen and foretold anyway. But this by no means diminishes the tension: one can in fact get greater tension in seeing how an inevitable disaster finally occurs than in following events in ignorance of the outcome until the very end.

Satan progresses, carrying 'hell within him'. Looking now towards Eden, clearly in his view, and now towards Heaven and the sun, he addresses the sun in terms that reveal the frustrations and contradictions of his inner state, ending his tortured soliloquy with the desperate cry 'Evil be thou my Good'. The speech is both morally and psychologically interesting, showing a complex relationship between suffering, guilt, pride and despair. It is also full of contradictions and shows the logical confusion to which acknowledged yet stubbornly unrepentant guilt may be led. Satan continues his progress towards the ideal landscape of Eden, in describing which Milton shows how effectively he could use elemental images:

> And higher than that Wall a circling row
> Of goodliest Trees loaden with fairest Fruit,
> Blossoms and Fruit at once of golden hue
> Appeard, with gay enameld colours mixt:
> On which the Sun more glad impress'd his beams
> Than in fair Evening Cloud, or humid Bow,
> When God hath showrd the earth; so lovely seemd
> That Lantskip: . . .

The culminating phrase, split between one line and the next, rings out in eloquent fullness: 'So lovely seemd that Lantskip'. 'Lovely' takes on a rich emotional charge by its positioning: spoiled though it has been for us by over-use in untold numbers of ordinary conversations, it retains its eloquence here, showing (as Gerard Manley Hopkins also demonstrated) that worn-out words can be permanently charged and re-charged with meaning when put in an appropriate verbal and rhythmic context.

As we keep our eyes on Satan we see him changing from the great fallen angel to the sly tempter of folklore. He is compared to a prowling wolf 'Watching where Shepherds pen thir Flocks at eeve' and to 'a Thief bent to unhoord the cash / Of some rich Burgher', images appealing respectively to the countryman and the city dweller, and, further, images taken from the familiar postlapsarian human world we know. This is the Devil whom preachers warn against, the familiar Devil of daily life and routine warning. And he is no longer grand. After the comparison with a sheep-stealing wolf and a city thief we find the deliberately denigrating line 'So clomb this first grand Thief into Gods Fould'.

Satan sits 'like a Cormorant' on the Tree of Life and we view the scene in Eden, again through his eyes. Milton draws on all his resources and a great range of classical and other references to build up this picture of the ideal garden, until the scene almost bursts with its own richness and beauty. This is *natural* beauty, not planted by 'nice Art' in 'Beds and curious Knots' but poured profusely out by Nature. Here all human dreams of ideal beauty in nature were actually realized. The trees bore fruit that were 'Hesperian Fables true,/If true, here only, and of delicious taste.' The Greek concept of Pan, the myth of the Graces, and story of Ceres and Proserpine, are brought in to give tremulous intensity to the picture:

> The Birds thir quire apply; aires, vernal aires,
> Breathing the smell of field and grove, attune
> The trembling leaves, while Universal *Pan*
> Knit with the *Graces* and the *Hours* in dance
> Led on th' Eternal Spring. Not that faire field
> Of *Enna*, where *Proserpin* gathering flours
> Her self a fairer Floure by gloomie *Dis*
> Was gatherd, which cost *Ceres* all that pain
> To seek her through the world; nor that sweet Grove
> Of *Daphne* by *Orontes*, and th' inspir'd
> *Castalian* Spring, might with this Paradise
> Of *Eden* strive; . . .

Finally, the camera, which has already climbed up over Eden's steep sides and then roved round the luxuriance of the garden, picks out (but again the lens is Satan's eye) the great prelapsarian couple, the only man and woman ever to have walked in complete innocence and true human dignity. One cannot

stress too much Milton's concept of the wonder of Adam and Eve before the
Fall. Looking back on an ideal unfallen man and woman from this fallen
world, he was conscious of having to use all his poetic powers to make them
convincing and persuasive, better than human as we know human yet at the
same time recognizably human:

> Two of far nobler shape erect and tall,
> Godlike erect, with native Honour clad
> In naked Majestie seemd Lords of all,
> And worthie seemd, for in thir looks Divine
> The image of thir glorious Maker shon,
> Truth, wisdome, Sanctitude severe and pure,
> Severe but in true filial freedom plac't; . . .

Milton emphasizes their nakedness, the lack of any sense of shame in
unfallen sexuality. In describing their surroundings — luxuriant nature and
animals frolicking in happy innocence and mutual amity — Milton draws on
a long tradition of visual representations of the Garden of Eden, but his touch
is his own. The almost baroque sense of luxuriance is controlled by a heraldic
formality:

> About them frisking play'd
> All Beasts of th' Earth, since wilde, and of all chase
> In Wood or Wilderness, Forrest or Den;
> Sporting the Lion rampd, and in his paw
> Dandl'd the Kid; Bears, Tygers, Ounces, Pards,
> Gambold before them, th' unwieldy Elephant
> To make them mirth us'd all his might, and wreathd
> His Lithe Proboscis; close the Serpent sly
> Insinuating, wove with Gordian twine
> His breaded train, and of his fatal guile
> Gave proof unheeded; others on the grass
> Couch't, and now fild with pasture gazing sat,
> Or Bedward ruminating; . . .

There follows a description of sunset in Paradise that combines a sense of
beauty and of wonder with a sense of awe at the cosmic dimensions involved:

> Mean while in utmost Longitude, where Heav'n
> With Earth and Ocean meets, the setting Sun
> Slowly descended, and with right aspect
> Against the eastern Gate of Paradise
> Leveld his eevning Rayes: . . .

Before this, however, we see Satan, gazing unseen at the happy pair, tortur-
ing himself with envy, mingling confused thoughts of pity for them, in view
of the fate he plans for them, pity for himself, and self-justification. He is
going to bring them to share his damnation because he is compelled by

'public reason just, Honour and Empire', which of course is complete nonsense. From the confused malign speech of Satan we turn to the noble simplicity of Adam's utterance. His speech, beginning with the words 'Sole partner and sole part of all these joyes/Dearer thy self then all', is worth studying for its smooth-flowing dignity. It is not at all rhetorical in the sense that Satan's speech is rhetorical; it represents Milton's conception of the speech of prelapsarian man. It is interesting that when Milton lets us for the first time hear Adam speaking to Eve, he is talking about the forbidden tree. It is an obsessive subject, to Adam, to Eve and indeed to God. Adam adjured Eve not to 'think hard one easy prohibition', thus giving away to eavesdropping Satan what that prohibition is, and Satan can therefore proceed with his plan to ruin them. Eve's reply has the same accents of loving courtesy as Adam's speech, but its tone is perhaps more liquid, more feminine. In describing, with a sense of innocent wonder, how she felt immediately after waking from her birth, she is possibly giving the reader an anticipation of her eventual succumbing to Satan's appeal to her vanity in her account of how she almost fell in love with her own image in a lake before she was led to discover that Adam was her mate. But this is not stressed. So far all is love and primal innocence, and Satan, watching with 'jealous leer malign', finds the sight hateful and tormenting. But he now knows how to set about destroying their happiness: to incite them to eat of the forbidden fruit of the Tree of Knowledge. For the first time in the poem a sense of the paradox of knowledge surfaces: Satan says that he will excite in the minds of Adam and Eve 'more desire to know', and that will lead them to disobedience. Yet without knowledge Adam and Eve, for all their beauty and grace and mutual courtesy, remain in a deep sense unfulfilled, as Milton conceded and as emerges elsewhere in the poem. But the matter is not explored further at this point.

Meanwhile the angels are exercising in 'heroic games' (a feature of the epic tradition that Milton felt obliged to include). Uriel warns Gabriel, who has been appointed by God to watch over the Garden of Eden lest any evil thing approach and enter, about Satan's journey (but it is all meaningless, since God foreknows and has already announced to the angels that Satan will enter and man will fall), and Gabriel assures him of his vigilance. Sunset is by now further advanced, and we get a splendid description of evening in Paradise:

Now came still Eevning on, and Twilight gray
Had in her sober Liverie all things clad;
Silence accompanied, for Beast and Bird,
They to thir grassie Couch, these to thir Nests
Were slunk, all but the wakeful Nightingale;
She all night long her amorous descant sung;
Silence was pleas'd: now glow'd the Firmament
With living Saphirs: *Hesperus* that led

> The starrie Host, rode brightest, till the Moon
> Rising in clouded Majestie, at length
> Apparent Queen unvaild her peerless light,
> And o're the dark her Silver Mantle threw.

Adam and Eve then talk to each other, again with that high but simple courtesy that marks their speech. They discuss labour and repose, and in doing so illustrate Milton's dilemma in having to accept the view expressed in Genesis that labour was a curse imposed on man as a punishment after the Fall. Adam explains that 'Man hath his daily work of body or mind/Appointed, which declares his Dignitie.' For Milton the daily round of labour and the thought of appointed work well done were always symbolic of all that was most satisfying in human experience: this is borne out by imagery that runs through all his poetry.

Eve's reply to Adam is couched in a language that has a lilt and balance that distinguish her speech from his. Her quietly eloquent expression of her love for her husband can almost be considered as a delicate love-lyric embodied in the text of the epic:

> Sweet is the breath of morn, her rising sweet
> With charm of earliest Birds; pleasant the Sun
> When first on this delightful Land he spreads
> His orient Beams, on herb, tree, fruit, and flour,
> Glistring with dew; fragrant the fertil earth
> After soft showers; and sweet the coming on
> Of grateful Eevning milde, then silent Night
> With this her solemn Bird and this fair Moon,
> And these the Gemms of Heav'n, her starrie train:
> But neither breath of Morn when she ascends
> With charm of earliest Birds, nor rising Sun
> On this delightful land, nor herb, fruit, floure,
> Glistring with dew, nor fragrance after showers,
> Nor grateful Eevning mild, nor silent Night
> With this her solemn Bird, nor walk by Moon,
> Or glittering Starr-light without thee is sweet.

The theme here — that nature is beautiful but without the loved one its beauty is meaningless — is a stock theme in poetry, from the medieval lyric to modern popular song, but it is its elemental nature that makes it so appropriate as an expression of this primal and innocent love. The quiet balance of the speech just quoted, with the catalogue of natural beauties repeated in the second half, is a simple but highly effective structural device.

The prelapsarian love of Adam and Eve is innocent, but for Milton innocence does not mean free from sexual pleasure. Milton is determined to make clear his view of innocent sexuality, contrasted with mere lust on the one hand and on the other with the artificial sighings and servitudes of the courtly love tradition. It is here that Milton gives us the strongest expression of his view of the place of sex in human relations and makes abundantly clear that such a view is far from what is conventionally labelled Puritan.

The poet then turns to contemplate the sleeping lovers:

> These lulld by Nightingales imbraceing slept,
> And on their naked limbs the flourie roof
> Showrd Roses, which the Morn repair'd. Sleep on
> Blest pair; and O yet happiest if ye seek
> No happier state, and know to know no more.

Milton is clearly deeply moved by his own imagination of the sleeping innocent lovers. This is what human love might have been. This is what Adam and Eve and all their descendants were to lose as a result of the eating of the fatal apple. Milton contemplates the pair in a mood of admiring benediction. But he knows that this is the last night of innocent love that they will spend, and we almost hear the catch in his throat, his sense of loss and might-have-been, in the lines that begin 'Sleep on, Blest pair'.

The account that follows, of Gabriel, Uzziel, Ithuriel and Zephon arranging to guard against any intrusion into the Garden of Eden is again part of that shadow-boxing that is inevitable when the story that unfolds is one whose outcome has been foreknown and predicted by the creator of all the characters involved. And the turn to Satan, whom the angels find 'Squat like a Toad, close at the eare of Eve', sounds stagey and hollow after the grand simplicities of the scene with Adam and Eve. Satan squats by Eve's ear in the form of a toad in order to give her corrupting dreams. When he is discovered by Gabriel, his scornful and arrogant reply ('Not to know mee argues your selves unknown') sounds forced and theatrical, as it is meant to. Gabriel punctuates Satan's rhetoric with a sharp exposure of his contradictions. The mutual abuse that follows is more in the style of the polemical pamphlets Milton wrote in his years as a political pamphleteer though it is done with great command of flexible versification as well as rhetorical devices – movement of lines, placing of pauses, use of sardonic questions and ironic remarks. The problem here was how to bring the dispute to an end. An epic combat between Gabriel and Satan would have been wholly inappropriate at this stage, so Milton decides to close the argument with a curious image, derived from both Homer and Isaiah, of God weighing Satan's lot in the celestial balances, where it is shown to be the lighter:

> The Fiend lookt up and knew
> His mounted scale aloft: nor more; but fled
> Murmuring, and with him fled the shades of night.

On this note of sullen darkness and foreboding Book IV comes to an end. The modern reader may be left with the teasing thought that if God could intervene so effectively to demonstrate His power over Satan simply by showing him weighing lighter in a pair of balances, why should He have stood idly by and allowed Satan to corrupt His creation − not only man, but, as a result of the corruption of man, Nature as well? Perhaps it was a mistake for Milton to have allowed the possibility of this thought to emerge at this point. But then the thought is basic to the whole story, and in the end makes it richer in human significance than a mere theological argument could have been.

Books V–VI

The description of dawn in Paradise at the opening of Book V − it is the morning of the day after Satan's arrival there − is followed by an account of Adam's waking up from his night's sleep (it was an 'Aerie light' sleep, 'from pure digestion bred / And temperat vapors bland' − no hangovers in prelapsarian Eden). Eve's sleep, however, had been less light and airy, for Satan had been whispering in her ear, giving her a nightmare. Her account of this nightmare to Adam is one of the most remarkable passages in *Paradise Lost*, capturing with disturbing accuracy the authentic trance-like atmosphere of a bad dream. The abrupt transitions, the shifts of perspective, and finally the immense relief on waking to find that it was all a dream, are the true stuff of nightmare.

Adam comforts Eve, and then they join in 'unmediated' prayer, as good English Puritans always did, for 'set' prayers were anathema to them. But just as the spontaneous prayers of English (and Scottish) Puritans were in fact very likely to be a tissue of echoes and recollections of Scriptural phrases, so Adam and Eve's prayer is largely built on verses 2–4 and 8–10 of Psalm 148 with echoes of psalm 19 and of the Canticle *Benedicite, omnia opera* (set for Matins in Lent in the 1549 Book of Common Prayer but not, of course, used consciously by English Puritans in their own worship). The elemental imagery of the prayer helps to give a sense of the wonder of the created cosmos, while at the same time the imagery modulates from grand themes such as the planets and the winds to the more intimate imagery of earth, trees, plants, hills, valleys and fountains. God looks down on the praying couple *with pity* − a remarkable admission by Milton: God pities the imminent fate of the creatures He created, which seems to imply that that fate is not wholly their fault. As though knowing that He could prevent it if He wanted, God then embarks on further discussion with Raphael about free will and responsibility.

God sends Raphael to warn Adam against the plotting of Satan, not so much to prevent the Fall (for, to repeat it once again, this was foreknown by God from the beginning) but to make sure that Adam had no excuse and could not pretend 'Surprisal, unadmonisht, unforwarnd'. In other words, Raphael's visit is really to make Adam more guilty when he does transgress and so more worthy of punishment. Whether this helps to justify the ways of God to men is another matter.

Raphael's descent to Eden gives Milton another opportunity to describe prelapsarian Nature —

> for Nature here
> Wantond as in her prime, and plaid at will
> Her Virgin Fancies, pouring forth more sweet,
> Wilde above Rule or Art; enormous bliss —

before he goes on to give an account of the encounter between the archangel and unfallen Adam. The picture of primal man, in all the dignity of innocent nakedness, greeting an angelic guest is done with simple dignity which Milton himself contrasts with the 'tedious pomp' of postlapsarian ceremony. Eve, too, in her innocent and naked beauty plays her part in this impressive scene. There is a kind of rank at work here. Raphael as an archangel is above Adam, and Adam, as the first created of humans, is above Eve. At the same time each has his or her special claim to distinction. Adam bows low to Raphael, but he is not awed. He is 'our Primitive great Sire', the first Man, and Raphael, though an archangel and as such Adam's superior, is only one among many. Eve is unique, her naked female beauty (Milton keeps emphasizing this) 'more lovely fair' than any woman ever imagined in later mythology. The conversation between Adam and Raphael, full of respectful attention on the one hand and of friendly advice and information on the other, shows how flexibly Milton could handle his blank verse in discussion and exposition (as opposed to argument, where he can be less happy). But when Raphael comes to tell of the war in Heaven, in the latter part of Book V and in Book VI, the inadequacy of the epic model for dealing with God's relation with His creatures is seen most clearly. Arms and armour, courageous deeds of arms, spectacular warfare, attacks and woundings and advances and retreats, are all described with great technical assurance. Angelologists have assured us that in showing the capacity of angels to be wounded (though not killed) Milton is following one of the accepted views about the angelic nature. Further, we know that this retrospective description of conflict, after the poem has opened at a later stage in the action *in medias res*, is in the established epic tradition going back to Homer. But for all the knowledge and the skill and indeed the ingenuity employed by Milton in his description of the battle between the loyal angels and their rebel opponents, most modern readers feel the whole of the action to be somewhat empty. God finally sends his Son to drive the rebels down to the place prepared for them, and the Son, mission accomplished, returns triumphantly to sit at God's right hand in Heaven to the sound of victory hymns by the angels. God of course could have driven the rebels down at the beginning, without any battle; or he could simply have *willed* them to retreat. Purposive action against odds aimed at achieving a desired but not certain result is appropriate to all other epics; but in dealing with a crisis involving the omnipotent and all-foreseeing Creator who actually created in the first place all the other characters involved in the action and retains total power over them, it is meaningless.

Raphael concludes his account – which is by way of being an awful warning to Adam of the dangers of rebellion against God – by saying that he has told it 'measuring things in heaven by things on earth'. Perhaps it was not really like that, Milton is implying, but this is the only way the human imagination can be brought to understand it. But there is something strange here. Adam and Eve were the first of humankind. They knew absolutely nothing of arms and armour, of battles and victories and defeats. How could they have benefited by being told of the struggle in Heaven in terms of the subsequent military history of fallen man? The answer presumably is that Milton is really telling the story to his readers, and the device of having Raphael tell it to Adam is an old established epic tradition where the hero narrates a whole section of his past history ostensibly to a newly found auditor, but really to the audience of the epic.

Books VII–VIII

At the beginning of Book VII Milton gathers up his forces to begin the second half of his epic ('Half yet remains unsung'). As always in entering on a new phase of the poem, he begins with an invocation, as he had done at the opening of the poem and at the beginning of Book III and as he will do at the beginning of Book IX. For the first time he now names his Muse, invoking her as Urania, but Milton goes on to point out that the Urania whom he invokes is not one of the nine muses of Greek mythology (she was the ancient Muse of Astronomy, appropriate enough for the cosmic scene Milton is about to describe) but a spiritual force akin to the divine wisdom that God employed in creating the universe. These invocations are always the most personal parts of the poem, and here Milton paints a vivid picture of himself, living blind in a hostile society, but sustained by his divine inspiration:

> Standing on Earth, not rapt above the Pole,
> More safe I Sing with mortal voice, unchang'd
> To hoarce or mute, though fall'n on evil dayes,
> On evil dayes though fall'n, and evil tongues;
> In darkness, and with dangers compast round,
> And solitude; yet not alone, while thou
> Visit'st my slumbers Nightly, or when Morn
> Purples the East: still govern thou my Song,
> *Urania*, and fit audience find though few.

The verse throbs with a kind of personal feeling unknown in the classical epic (notice, for example, the repetition, with inversion, of 'though fall'n on evil Dayes' and the threefold use of the word 'evil') and conveys something of the profound sense of mission with which Milton approached his self-imposed talk of writing the great Christian epic. It also conveys his sense of isolation in a wicked world.

The account that the archangel Raphael gives to Adam of the Creation is not the most original part of *Paradise Lost*, being inevitably based on the Genesis story, which Milton was committed to taking as a literal source, but also blending in other biblical sources and Platonic and other notions. The descriptive writing can be impressive, and the imagery is often arresting in its combination of stylized movement with heraldic colour and form:

> The grassie Clods now Calv'd, now half appeer'd
> The Tawnie Lion, pawing to get free
> His hinder parts, then springs as broke from Bonds,
> And Rampant shakes his Brinded main; the Ounce,
> The Libbard, and the Tyger, as the Moale
> Rising, the crumbl'd Earth above them threw
> In Hillocks; the swift Stag from under ground
> Bore up his branching head: . . .

Raphael prefaces his account of the Creation by explaining why God decided on it in the first place. It was to repair the damage done by the fall of the rebel angels:

> I can repaire
> That detriment, if such it be to lose
> Self-lost, and in a moment will create
> Another World, out of one man a Race
> Of men innumerable, there to dwell,
> Not here, till by degrees of merit rais'd
> They open to themselves at length the way
> Up hither, under long obedience tri'd,
> And Earth be chang'd to Heav'n, & Heav'n to Earth,
> One Kingdom, Joy and Union without end.

But as God foreknew from the beginning all that would happen, He must have known perfectly well that Satan would interfere with his plan, and that it would as a result miscarry, and in the end only a tiny minority of mortals attain salvation. Once again we are faced with the paradox of having an omniscient and omnipotent divine power put in a situation of planning and supposing and allowing for contingencies, a situation only too appropriate for mortal man but wholly inappropriate to Divinity. There is simply no way out of this problem for Milton; if he is to write an epic on the subject he has chosen, he has no option but to ignore it and carry on. (One might add that much of the Bible, as Milton reminds us in his *Christian Doctrine*, also

presents God as planning, contriving, regretting, hoping, and so on, but
then the Bible does not bring in sophisticated arguments about the con-
sistency of foreknowledge of God with freewill in man and it would never
have entered into the head of any of the authors of the Bible that God needed
justification. True, the Bible accepts – or some parts of it do – that God's
ways are mysterious, but then, as is made clear in the Book of Job, this just
has to be accepted as part of the wonder of a universe largely impenetrable to
human understanding. Milton will not accept any mystery; everything has
to be cleared up with convincing logic; and this is really his trouble.)

Milton's own prose 'argument' prefixed to Book VII explains that in the
first part of that book 'Adam inquires concerning celestial Motions, is doubt-
fully answer'd, and exhorted to search things rather more worthy of
knowledg'. The Humanist and the Christian are not wholly reconciled in the
arguments presented by Raphael. Milton's dilemma is of course far from
original with him and he employs the long familiar distinction between vain
knowledge and proper knowledge, which was self-knowledge. Milton is
careful not to commit himself as between the different astronomical systems
known in the seventeenth century, and Raphael's account is full of hypo-
thetical questions and suppositions ('What if that light . . . be as a Starr
. . .?' '. . . other suns perhaps with thir attendant Moons . . .', 'but
whether thus these things or whether not', 'What if the Sun be Center to
the World?'). This is hardly satisfactory as an account of the nature of the
universe given by a being of angelic intelligence, and it illustrates Milton's
dilemma in trying to use his human skills in conveying superhuman
knowledge. In the end Adam is adjured not to dream of other worlds and to
live contented with the doubtful information about the cosmos that has been
revealed to him.

Adam, at Raphael's request, then gives an account of his first days on
earth. Raphael wants to know because, as he quite simply explains, he
happened to be absent on the day of Adam's creation, 'bound on a voyage
uncouth and obscure'. Raphael's absence on divine business at this interesting time is characteristic of the lively and charming touches in this part of
Book VIII, one of the most attractive being the conversation between God
and Adam on the question of a mate. God and Adam are talking in Eden, and
Adam complains of his solitude. The bright vision of God 'as with a smile
more bright'nd' and replies that Adam is not really solitary at all:

> is not the Earth
> With various living creatures, and the Aire
> Replenisht, and all these at thy command
> To come and play before thee, . . .?

Adam replies humbly but firmly that animals are not his equals, and 'Among
unequals what societie/Can sort, what harmonie or true delight?' God's
reply to this is a piece of engagingly humorous teasing:

A nice and suttle happiness I see
Thou to thy self proposest, in the choice
Of thy Associates, *Adam*, and wilt taste
No pleasure, though in pleasure, solitarie.
What thinkst thou then of mee, and this my State,
Seem I to thee sufficiently possest
Of happiness, or not? who am alone
From all Eternitie, for none I know
Second to me or like, equal much less.

Adam is not quite sure whether he is being teased or not, but he plays safe and answers God's argument with humble patience: man's position is really very different from God's and God's comparison proves nothing. God lets Adam run on before pointing out that he had been only teasing all the time. He knew that it was not good for man to be alone (Milton is echoing Genesis here, but in a very different mood) and had already planned a mate for him. The half-humorous anthropomorphism here is more attractive than the more ambitious anthropomorphism of the scenes in Heaven.

Adam then gives Raphael an account of his feelings when he was first presented with Eve: it is an account throbbing with passion and sensuality (Eve, we are specifically told, was created with full knowledge of 'nuptial sanctity and marriage Rites'). His sense of weakness before 'the charm of Beauties powerful glance' is conveyed with a conviction that makes it clear that Milton was drawing on his own experience (we know from other sources that in spite of his dedicatedly chaste life as a young man he was very highly sexed and knew what it was to be swept off his feet by sexual desire). There is distinct foreshadowing of Adam's later action in following Eve in eating the fatal apple when he tells Raphael that

All higher wisdom in her presence falls
Degraded, Wisdom in discourse with her
Looses discount'nanc't, and like folly shewes; . . .

This upsets Raphael, whose brow contracts as he warns Adam sternly against allowing his reason to be subdued by sexual passion: 'In loving thou dost well, in passion not'.

Milton is not here making a distinction between love and sex, for to him sex was right and proper in a marriage relationship, and he goes out of his way to have Raphael tell Adam that angels enjoy sexual union in Heaven, mingling more totally than mortals can. The distinction is between true love (which involves sex) and irrational passion. Discussions of the various kinds of love, sacred and profane, were common enough in the Renaissance, and many poets as well as philosophers treated the subject (Spenser was one). Here however the question is not so much discussed as presented dramatically. There is real tension in the confrontation between Adam and Raphael.

Adam is 'half abash't' by Raphael's reproof, and points out with moving simplicity that it is not simply sexual intercourse with Eve that gives him pleasure (though he does not undervalue that) but

> Those thousand decencies that daily flow
> From all her words and actions mixt with Love
> And sweet compliance, with declare unfeign'd
> Union of Mind, or in us both one Soule;
> Harmonie to behold in wedded pair
> More grateful than harmonious sound to the eare.

This is what Milton had pleaded for in his divorce pamphlets. It was an ideal to be rudely tested by Satan's temptation.

Book IX

Book IX is the greatest of the books of *Paradise Lost*. The opening indicates Milton's own sense of doom in contemplating what is to come:

> No more of talk where God or Angel Guest
> With Man, as with his Friend, familiar us'd
> To sit indulgent, and with him partake
> Rural repast, permitting him the while
> Venial discourse unblam'd: I now must change
> Those Notes to Tragic; foul distrust, and breach
> Disloyal on the part of Man, revolt,
> And disobedience: On the part of Heav'n
> Now alienated, distance and distaste,
> Anger and just rebuke, and judgement giv'n,
> That brought into this World a world of woe,
> Sinne and her shadow Death, and Miserie
> Deaths harbinger: . . .

A sad task, he goes on, but one far more truly heroic than the themes of ancient Greek or Latin epic. He goes on to list in contemptuous detail the standard properties of both ancient and Renaissance epic, 'Races and Games, / Or tilting Furniture, emblazon'd Shields, / Impresses quaint, Caparisons and Steeds' and so on and on. The 'better fortitude / Of Patience and Heroic Martyrdom' remained unsung, but the epic he is now writing will remedy that, if only his divine inspiration does not fail; if only, 'long choosing and beginning late', he has not delayed too long to find himself in 'an age too late' or too cold a climate; if only his 'Celestial Patroness' will inspire him with an 'answerable style' appropriate to his great venture. In this mixture of confidence and doubt, with a final autobiographical outburst, Milton approaches the central scene of his tragic epic.

Satan has come back to Eden (having been temporarily driven out by Gabriel) and enters into the serpent ('subtlest Beast of all the Field') in order to disguise himself. The characterization of the serpent comes from Genesis, and Milton is bound by this text, though he accepts the later tradition that it was not the serpent itself but Satan in the serpent that tempted Eve. Before actually entering the serpent Satan delivers himself of a speech which shows his further degeneration into a spiteful destroyer who finds ease only in destruction, which brings him revenge even if revenge 'bitter ere long back on itself recoils'. He is cutting off his nose to spite his face. After a description of dawn in Eden, we turn to Adam and Eve and find them engaged in a sweetly courteous difference of opinion. Eve, presumably because of a suggestion put into her mind by Satan when he squatted by her ear in the form of a toad while she slept, suggests to Adam that they divide their labours and work in different parts of the garden. The reason she gives is interesting:

> For while so near each other thus all day
> Our taske we choose, what wonder if so near
> Looks intervene and smiles, or objects new
> Casual discourse draw on, which intermits
> Our dayes work brought to little, though begun
> Early, and th' hour of Supper comes unearn'd.

The idea of having to earn supper by work is postlapsarian, since the necessity to earn his bread by labour was part of the curse laid on man as a punishment for the Fall, but, as we have seen in other instances, Milton was unable to imagine a workless world as providing any satisfaction. Or is there perhaps a suggestion here that Eve's mind is already tainted with a postlapsarian thought?

The pair are, however, still unfallen, and their difference of opinion is presented in a discourse full of that quiet grace that Milton always introduced into his verse when describing their behaviour and conversation before eating the fatal apple. When Adam finally consents, reluctantly, to let Eve go, knowing that 'thy stay, not free, absents thee more', there is the suggestion that Eve, having won her point, does not really want to act on it and she goes only because her previous insistence makes it necessary that she should. There is almost an air of fatalism here. Eve is driven by something beyond herself to insist on working separately from Adam, and Adam consents out of his love for her. There is no way in which we feel, at this stage, that Eve is to blame for her desire to work in a different part of the garden. But it is all part of Satan's plan.

The two part reluctantly, and as Eve slowly slides her hand out of her husband's Milton uses the richest resources of classical mythology (in a passage quoted earlier) to dwell for the last time on her innocence and beauty. The string of classical comparisons is drawn out, as though Milton, like Adam, is reluctant to see Eve go. Adam charges her again and again to be back by noon, and again and again she promises that she will:

A + E — trapped by their own innocence

> Oft he to her his charge of quick returne
> Repeated, shee to him as oft engag'd
> To be returnd by Noon amid the Bowre,
> And all things in best order to invite
> Noontide repast, or Afternoons repose.

She will be back to make lunch for them both, in fact. The knowledge that she will not return to make lunch, that that was the great tragically uneaten lunch of history, overcomes Milton at this stage. For he knows that although Eve will eventually return, it will not be the Eve that had left, not the Eve, lovely and gentle in her innocent nakedness, who had discoursed so sweetly with Adam before. Instead of making Adam's noontide repast she had eaten the forbidden apple, which Adam would then eat too, and everything would be changed. Milton's lingering on this final moment when prelapsarian man and woman stand hand in hand for the last time produces its own plangent emotion, which he can hardly control. He bursts out:

> O much deceav'd, much failing, hapless *Eve*,
> Of thy presum'd return! event perverse!
> Thou never from that houre in Paradise
> Foundst either sweet repast, or sound repose;
> Such ambush hid among sweet Flours and Shades
> Waited with hellish rancour imminent
> To intercept thy way, or send thee back
> Despoild of innocence, of Faith, of Bliss.

The verse cannot but make us feel that Eve is to be entrapped in a fiendishly contrived ambush, entrapped by her innocence and lack of knowledge, and that the blame that Milton has to believe attaches itself to her is misdirected. It is as though the tone of the narrative is at odds with Milton's theological intention.

The paradox is highlighted by the temptation scene itself. Eve is 'our credulous mother': she believes the serpent because she has no reason not to. She has never encountered evil; she has not yet eaten of the fruit of the tree of good and evil, so how could she be suspicious of the serpent, whom she takes to be simply a serpent telling the truth, when he tells her what has happened to him as a result of his eating of that fruit? It is, as it were, a Catch-22 situation: Eve could not be suspicious of the serpent, could not therefore resist him, unless she knew about hypocrisy and lying. But she could not know about hypocrisy and lying without having actually eaten of the forbidden fruit. It is true that one could say that she had been warned by a divine command not to eat it and therefore her prime duty was simply to obey that command. But if what the serpent said was true, the whole situation had to be looked at differently and Eve in her innocence *had* to believe that what the serpent said was true. Her fault here was credulity (as Milton admitted) and lack of suspicion. But is it morally evil to be over trustful?

Satan's eloquence in persuading Eve to eat of the forbidden fruit is compared by Milton to the speech of 'som Orator renownd / In Athens or free Rome', which is a pretty high tribute to its persuasiveness (although, as we have seen, Milton had by now come to be suspicious of classical rhetoric). If Eve had known more — a very great deal more — she would have been suspicious of this marvellously plausible eloquence. But she could not know while still unfallen. So she is persuaded, she eats, she falls, and Adam, desiring to share her fate out of love for her, eats too. So he falls as well and all mankind falls with him. And this tragedy is played out by creatures whom God had created, foreseeing that it would all happen. 'O much deceav'd, much failing, hapless Eve!' Much deceived and hapless, certainly. Failing too, in the sense that she allowed herself to be deceived, but as we read the moving account of how it happened in Milton's throbbing words, can we say that the poetry finds her blameworthy? Should we not rather say that, in a sense in spite of himself, Milton is here exploring, or at least presenting, a daring moral paradox, which has to do with the relation between innocence and virtue? If we can only resist evil by knowing it, and if we can only know it by becoming involved in it, then the innocent are incapable of true virtue and only the morally tarnished can in the end succeed in the struggle for true virtue. What philosophers call the conative theory of virtue — the view that virtue can be achieved only by struggle against odds — is incompatible with the view that true innocence can achieve it. So, we might say, the Fall was necessary if true virtue was to become possible for man. It might have been better of course, if man continued innocent and ignorant, unable to achieve that kind of hard-won virtue. But Milton did not really believe that. If Eve falls through the credulity of innocence, Adam falls through his love for Eve. This does not mean that in following Eve's example he is shown as doing right. The duty of an unfallen man who wants to help an unfallen beloved is not to share her sin, and so condemn them both, but to intercede for her while he himself is still sinless. It is not through passion that Adam follows Eve in eating the apple, but as the result of a considered decision to share her fate. Eve receives this service in the true Courtly Love tradition, which Milton is here parodying, when she delightedly accepts it as a 'glorious trial of exceeding Love'. To perform difficult and dangerous tasks set by the beloved was part of the Courtly Love code, which Milton rejected on two grounds, first that it was not man's place to obey a woman ('Was she thy God, that her thou didst obey?' God later harshly asks Adam) and secondly that as the act itself involved disobedience to an express divine command no other authority could authorize it. Once the apple had been tasted, the couple become irresponsible and fatuous. Eve had changed as soon as she had eaten it, bowing to the tree in drunken worship, and spilling out her story to Adam, when she finally returns to the bower, with the most brilliant of all 'Sorry I'm late, but —' speeches in English poetry.

    Hast thou not wonderd, *Adam*, at my stay?
Thee I have misst, and thought it long, depriv'd
Thy presence, agonie of love till now
Not felt, nor shall be twice, for never more
Mean to trie, what rash untri'd I sought,
The pain of absence from thy sight. But strange
Hath bin the cause, and wonderful to heare:
This Tree is not as we are told, a Tree
Of danger tasted, nor to evil unknown
Op'ning the way, but of Divine effect
To open Eyes, and make them Gods who taste;
And hath bin tasted such: the Serpent wise,
Or not restraind as wee, or not obeying,
Hath eat'n of the fruit, and is become,
Not dead, as we are threatn'd, but thenceforth
Endu'd with human voice and human sense,
Reasoning to admiration, and with mee
Perswasively hath so prevaild, that I
Have also tasted, and have also found
Th' effects to correspond, opener mine Eyes,
Dimm erst, dilated Spirits, ampler Heart,
And growing up to Godhead; which for thee
Chiefly I sought, without thee can despise.
For bliss, as thou hast part, to me is bliss,
Tedious, unshar'd with thee, and odious soon.
Thou therefore also taste, that equal Lot
May joyne us, equal Joy, as equal Love;
Least thou not tasting, different degree
Disjoyne us, and I then too late renounce
Deitie for thee, when Fate will not permit.

This speech, with its tumbling rush of words and breathless, drunken lilt,
is sharply distinguished from the gentle, liquid tones of Eve before her Fall.
Milton emphasizes the flushed excitement: 'Thus *Eve* with Countenance
blithe her storie told,/But in her Cheek distemper flushing glowd.' There is
a powerful dramatic picture of Adam, smitten by horror, letting fall from his
slack hand the garland of roses he had woven for Eve while awaiting her
return:

    On th' other side, *Adam*, soon as he heard
The fatal Trespass don by *Eve*, amaz'd,
Astonied stood and Blank, while horror chill
Ran through his veins, and all his joynts relax'd;
From his slack hand the Garland wreath'd for *Eve*
Down drop'd, and all the faded Roses shed:

This is a situation exploited again and again in later stories and in Holywood
films: the lover prepares something special for his beloved while awaiting

her, and she does not turn up. In this case Eve eventually does turn up, but it is a different Eve. Adam replies to Eve's drunken-sounding speech in tones of controlled dignity, for he is still unfallen; but gradually his love and compassion lead him to the conclusion that he must follow her example. He does not reproach her – reproaches only come after both have fallen – and his opening words are full of admiration and love:

> O fairest of Creation, last and best
> Of all Gods works, Creature in whom excell'd
> Whatever can to sight or thought be formd,
> Holy, divine, good, amiable, or sweet!
> How art thou lost, how on a sudden lost,
> Defac't, deflourd, and now to Death devote?
> Rather how hast thou yeelded to transgress
> The strict forbiddance, how to violate
> The sacred Fruit forbidd'n! som cursed fraud
> Of Enemie hath beguil'd thee, yet unknown,
> And mee with thee hath ruind, for with thee
> Certain my resolution is ιo Die;
> How can I live without thee, how forgoe
> Thy sweet Converse and Love so dearly joyn'd,
> To live again in these wilde Woods forlorn?
> Should God create another *Eve*, and I
> Another Rib afford, yet loss of thee
> Would never from my heart; no no, I feel
> The Link of Nature draw me: Flesh of Flesh,
> Bone of my Bone thou art, and from thy State
> Mine never shall be parted, bliss or woe.

The tone and structure of this speech are remarkable. Although we are clearly to understand that Adam has reached the wrong conclusion, it is difficult to put one's finger on the exact point where he went wrong. As an expression of tender love it is eloquent and moving. At the same time it reveals something of the paradox involved in loving another so much that one cannot bear not to share the loved one's fate. Is it the ultimate in selflessness or the ultimate in selfishness to sacrifice everything in order to spare oneself the agonizing experience of seeing one's beloved in a pain that one does not share? Love is a kind of egotism when the lovers feel as one and are pained by each other's pain. Milton was well aware that human experience involves many situations in which a man may be led astray even by his own virtues. It would be a harsh ethic that could fault Adam on this speech. Certainly to punish him and all his descendants in a most horrific way for acting on the decision he here arrives at seems appalling. But in a sense the punishment lies in the paradox of the situation. In the human condition as we know it, love is like that. One cannot fault Milton's psychological insight, which goes beyond the theological and logical boundaries of the poem. This may not justify the ways of God to men, but it makes the meaning of the Fall real in human terms.

Adam goes on to argue himself into a belief that God would not dare to destroy His own handiwork: that would simply be playing into the hands of His enemies (as indeed it was, but this did not prevent God from acting). Adam of course is deceiving himself, though the logic is sound enough. Logic, Milton shows, can lead astray as much as rhetoric. Then, on the twin grounds that he loves Eve too much not to want to share her fate and that God would not really carry out the threats He had made in the event of their disobeying His order not to eat of the fruit of the tree of Good and Evil, Adam too eats of the fatal apple. The change this works in him is as immediate as the change that had been wrought in Eve, whom he now addresses in a nasty parody of the teasing tone in which God had spoken to him about a mate:

> *Eve*, now I see that thou art nice of taste,
> And elegant, of Sapience no small part,
> Since to each meaning savour we apply,
> And Palate call judicious; I the praise
> Yeild thee, so well this day thou hast purvey'd.

He goes on to say, in a mood of reckless levity and bravado, that if forbidden fruit is all as nice as this, 'it might be wish'd, / For this one Tree had been forbidden ten'. The reader's attitude towards him is no longer what it had been when he made the speech persuading himself to share Eve's fate because of his love for her. This is a fallen Adam, a much less sympathetic Adam, talking blasphemous nonsense.

Now, for the first time, sex becomes guilty. Images suggesting drunkenness and irresponsibility abound in Milton's account of the first postlapsarian sexual act. Adam and Eve awake from the restless sleep that follows with the wholly new knowledge of shame. A new kind of self-consciousness is present, and it destroys all their satisfaction in their mutual relationship. The pair bicker with sullen regret and mutual reproachfulness, speaking in tones worlds apart from those of their prelapsarian talk, and Book IX ends in mutual accusation:

> Thus they in mutual accusation spent
> The fruitless hours, but neither self-condemning,
> And of thir vain contest appeer'd no end.

Books X–XII

Book X opens with Milton reiterating, almost obsessively, that none of what happened was God's fault even though He was the omnipotent and omniscient creator of all the characters involved:

> what can scape the Eye
> Of God All-seeing, or deceave his Heart
> Omniscient, who in all things wise and just,
> Hinder'd not *Satan* to attempt the minde
> Of Man, with strength entire, and free will arm'd,
> Complete to have discover'd and repulst
> Whatever wiles of Foe or seeming Friend.
> For still they knew, and ought to have still remember'd
> The high Injunction not to taste that Fruit,
> Whoever tempted; which they not obeying,
> Incurr'd, what could they less, the penaltie,
> And manifold in sin, deserv'd to fall.

Adam and Eve '*ought* to have still remember'd', and that was that. But it is probably true that most readers, at least modern readers, have lost interest in this aspect of the poem, and are involved with the human situation of Adam and Eve. Less interesting, too, is the account of the changes that begin to take place on earth and in Hell as a consequence of the Fall. The poem's interest picks up at once when Milton begins to chart the process of recovery on the part of both Adam and Eve. At first Adam repels Eve with bitter anger:

> Out of my sight, thou Serpent, that name best
> Befits thee with him leagu'd, thy self as false
> And hateful; . . .

It is Eve who begins the process of recovery, in her beautifully modulated reply. The tone here is equally different from that of her prelapsarian speech and that of her speech immediately after eating the apple. It has an elegiac note, the quiet, sad cadence of experience, with balances and repetitions ('forsake me not . . . bereave me not . . . on me exercise not') and a new kind of humility:

> Forsake me not thus, Adam, witness Heav'n
> What love sincere, and reverence in my heart
> I beare thee, and unweeting have offended,
> Unhappilie deceav'd; thy suppliant
> I beg, and clasp thy knees; bereave me not,
> Whereon I live, thy gentle looks, thy aid,
> Thy counsel in this uttermost distress,
> My onely strength and stay: forlorn of thee,
> Whither shall I betake me, where subsist?
> While yet we live, scarse one short hour perhaps,
> Between us two let there be peace, both joyning,
> As joyn'd in injuries, one enmitie
> Against a Foe by doom express assign'd us,
> That cruel Serpent: On me exercise not
> Thy hatred for this miserie befall'n,

On me alreadie lost, mee then thy self
More miserable; both have sin'd, but thou
Against God onely, I against God and thee,
And to the place of judgment will return,
There with my cries importune Heaven, that all
The sentence from thy head remov'd may light
On me, sole cause to thee of all this woe,
Mee mee onely just object of his ire.

Adam responds to this remarkable speech — the first postlapsarian speech
to show signs of grace — with words of compassion and comfort: Eve's new
state of mind has now brought about his moral recovery too. From this point
on the pair's recovery develops — not in a straight line, for Milton knew too
much about human nature to imagine that that is how things happened, but
in a halting and winding manner, to end in their joint prayer to God of
submission and penitence.

The immediate punishment for the Fall, the curse of work to earn a living
and the pain of childbirth for women, is somewhat perfunctorily described
early in Book X. Milton is here content to follow the account in Genesis
without adding any resonance of his own. He is more interested in the
process of recovery in Adam and Eve. It is not even clear that Milton took the
double curse very seriously. Certainly work for him was no curse, and
Adam's light-hearted remark seems to represent his own view:

On mee the Curse aslope
Glanc'd on the ground, with labour I must earne
My bread; what harm? Idleness had bin worse; . . .

Milton indeed seems to be somewhat at a loss after the Fall has occurred until
he can return to Adam and Eve and chart their development. The horrid
changes brought about by the Fall are described vividly enough, but on a different level of interest altogether, while the spectacle of God watching from
Heaven 'these Dogs of Hell' advancing 'To waste and havoc yonder World,
which I / So fair and good created' does nothing to justify His ways. When
Milton has God say that He actually called and drew thither

My Hell-hounds, to lick up the draff and filth
Which mans polluting Sin with taint hath shed
On what was pure,

we feel that he is in a bit of a dilemma. There is in fact no good reason why
the omnipotent and omniscient God allowed these filthy monsters to pollute
the world He had created. It is of course presented as one of the consequences
of the eating of the fatal apple, as is the view, accepted by Adam himself in
one of the speeches made in the course of his recovery, that it is perfectly just
and proper that all his posterity should 'stand curst' because of his
transgression. True, he asks the obvious question

> Ah, why should all mankind
> For one man's fault thus guiltless be condemn'd,
> If guiltless?

But he answers, in Christian theological terms, 'But from me what can proceed,/But all corrupt, both Mind and Will deprav'd, . . .' It is not in this kind of argument that the true glory of *Paradise Lost* resides. We return with relief to Adam and Eve, follow their recovery, and leave them at the end of Book X praying in humble penitence.

The stern archangel Michael, very different from the 'affable' Raphael, is now sent down to Eden to narrate the future of the world to Adam. It is a thoroughly miserable story, told with a weary disgust, from Cain's committing the first murder to the final picture of the world going on 'To good malignant, to bad men benign' until the Day of Judgment. The story of Christ's passion and triumph, which breaks the dismal chronicle with a momentary gleam of light and elicits in Adam his great hail to the 'fortunate Fall' –

> O goodness infinite, goodness immense!
> That all this good of evil shall produce,
> And evil turn to good;

– is not, in the story as revealed by Michael, the culmination, but only an incident in the long history, and in some respects a less cheering incident than the quiet beauty of the picture of the earth returning to normal again after the flood, never again to be so overwhelmed:

> but when he brings
> Over the Earth a Cloud, will therein set
> His triple-colour'd Bow, whereon to look
> And call to mind his Cov'nant: Day and Night,
> Seed time and Harvest, Heat and hoary Frost
> Shall hold thir course, till fire purge all things new,
> Both Heav'n and Earth, wherein the just shall dwell.

For Milton the loss of Eden's perpetual spring, the consequent procession of seasons each with its appropriate work, could not really be a curse, but was a source of deep satisfaction. This is not presented in the poem as a conscious comfort, but it is there, echoing again and again in the imagery, so that one might almost say that it plays its part in a counter-poem which says that the Fall was a good thing because it enabled man to contend with knowledge against the forces of evil and to prove his worth in so contending and because it provided the satisfaction of work well accomplished, seasonal work for the agricultural labourer, intellectual work to the thinker, creative work to the poet. The dismal history of the world after the Fall, reflecting truly enough Milton's outlook on Restoration England, has to be read in the light of the pattern of suggestions built up by recurring imagery throughout the poem.

In the end Milton and Adam turn from grandiose public hopes to the 'paradise within', content with the prospect of 'with good/Still overcoming evil and by small/Accomplishing great things, . . .' In the fallen world, Michael tells Adam, tyranny is inevitable, 'though to the Tyrant thereby no excuse'. In spite of everything, the note of patience and purpose rises as the poem proceeds to its conclusion. In the end, the Garden of Eden, Paradise, becomes untenable, not only because God has made it so after driving Adam and Eve from it, but because mature man has no real use for a life of innocent lotus-eating. The world calls, with its challenge, its testing times, its terrible and wonderful paradoxes involving human love and companionship and loneliness. As the expelled couple look back, Eden looks simply terrifying. But before them lies the world; they are together, hand in hand yet solitary, for there is a core of solitary uniqueness in every individual and love is full of contradictions. The image of the labourer returning homeward in the evening sets the emotional tone of the concluding passage. 'The World was all before them'. Paradise may be Lost, but there is a world of purposive endeavour waiting to be tamed ('the subjected Plain' suggests both the plain lying below and the plain to be conquered by agricultural labour). It is a great and memorable ending:

> for now too nigh
> Th' Archangel stood, and from the other Hill
> To thir fixt Station, all in bright array
> The Cherubim descended; on the ground
> Gliding meteorous, as Ev'ning Mist
> Ris'n from a River o're the marish glides,
> And gathers ground fast at the Labourers heel
> Homeward returning. High in Front advanc't,
> The brandisht Sword of God before them blaz'd
> Fierce as a Comet; which with torrid heat,
> And vapour as the *Libyan* Air adust,
> Began to parch that temperate Clime; whereat
> In either hand the hastning Angel caught
> Our lingring Parents, and to th' Eastern Gate
> Led them direct, and down the Cliff as fast
> To the subjected Plaine; then disappeer'd.
> They looking back, all th' Eastern side beheld
> Of Paradise, so late thir happie seat,
> Wav'd over by that flaming Brand, the Gate
> With dreadful Faces throng'd and fierie Armes:
> Som natural tears they drop'd, but wip'd them soon;
> The World was all before them, where to choose
> Thir place of rest, and Providence thir guide:
> They hand in hand with wandring steps and slow,
> Through *Eden* took thir solitarie way.

Further Reading

There are a number of usefully annotated editions of individual books of *Paradise Lost*, but the most comprehensively annotated text of the whole poem available to students is that edited by Alastair Fowler in *The Poems of John Milton*, edited by John Carey and Alastair Fowler (London, 1968). Some helpful critical works are:

Broadbent, John B., *Some Graver Subject: An Essay on 'Paradise Lost'* (London, 1960).

Kermode, Frank (ed.), *The Living Milton* (London, 1960).

Lewis, C.S., *A Preface to 'Paradise Lost'* (London, 1942). (This brilliant but partial book finds Milton's justification of God to men wholly convincing. Another brilliant and partial book, written from an opposite point of view, might well be read alongside it: Empson, William, *Milton's God*, London, 1961).

Prince, F.T., *The Italian Element in Milton's Verse* (Oxford, 1954).

Rajan, B., *'Paradise Lost' and the Seventeenth Century Reader* (London, 1962).

Ricks, Christopher, *Milton's Grand Style* (Oxford, 1963).

Index